# Graffiti in the PAC 10

# GRAFFITI IN THE PAC TEN

## Marina N. Haan
## Richard B. Hammerstrom

**WARNER BOOKS**

A Warner Communications Company

**Copyright © 1981**
by Brown House Galleries, Ltd.

Warner Books, Inc.,
75 Rockefeller Plaza,
New York, N. Y. 10019

W A Warner Communications Company

Cover design by Gene Light

Cover art by Jack Davis

Artistic enhancement by Jerry Mymudes,
Marina Haan, and Richard Hammerstrom

**First printing: September 1981**

10  9  8  7  6  5  4  3  2

Printed in the United States of America


**Library of Congress Cataloging in Publication Data**
Haan, Marina N.
    Graffiti in the PAC Ten.

    1. Graffiti—West (U.S.)  2. College students—
West (U.S.)  3. Pacific Ten Conference.    I. Hammer-
strom, Richard B.    II. Title.
GT3913.W38H3        081        81–2866
                                AACR2

ISBN 0-446-37603-5 (U.S.A.)

# DEDICATION

*We dedicate this book to the student in the stall next door, whose unflinching singleness of purpose and unquestioning acceptance of deviant bathroom behavior have allowed us to pursue our research without disruption of the natural habitat.*

# AUTHORS' NOTE

It was becoming increasingly clear that all areas of the western portion of the United States were threatened with one sort of imminent destruction or another.

Recent investigations had indicated the probable long-term continuation and expansion of volcanic activity in the Northwest. The scientific community had predicted the inevitable arrival of a catastrophic earthquake the length of California. The onset of a massive water shortage hung over the Southwest.

There seemed little doubt that the entire region, from Washington to Arizona, was doomed. We voiced our concern in appropriate circles.

"So what," some said. "Who needs 'em? We can get sand from the Arabs, movies from the Italians, and timber from Norway."

"Now, wait," we answered. "There would certainly be a great loss if the entire culture of this area were to slip away unnoticed."

"Culture? What culture?" some retorted. "You're talking about people who live in hot, dry sand, in cold, wet mountains, and Los Angeles. What's to lose?"

Undaunted, we replied, "But there are the centers of learning to consider. There are the universities of the Pacific Ten Conference. Certainly they have a culture worth saving, a history worth recording, a statement worth passing on to future generations."

Some scoffed. "Oh, you think so," they said. "Well, then, why don't you go and find out?"

Challenged, we responded, "We will! That's exactly what we'll do!"

And so, being good citizens, we had become committed to a study of the culture of the universities of the PAC Ten.

Our initial investigations were troublesome. We went to all of the offices and officers, to all the libraries and librarians, to all of the proper places and people. Still, we could not find what we wanted.

Though there was a great deal of information maintained about the schools of the PAC Ten, it had to do with such things as foundings, fundings, and footballs. Nowhere could we find studies that spoke to the emotions of the university community, to the lives of the members of the community, to what might really be lost when disaster struck.

Then, quite by chance, Nature called, and we realized that we were surrounded by the research material that we needed—graffiti. In the graffiti of the PAC Ten was recorded the true nature of the Western cultures. Here, in anonymity and seclusion, people inscribed their basic feelings. Here we would discover and preserve the culture of the threatened areas.

With unbounded enthusiasm we thrust ourselves upon the universities of the PAC Ten. We searched every building, scoured every room, screened every writable surface. We found the PAC Ten. We found its innermost soul.

Our work is done now. We have gathered together the product of the PAC Ten graffitiists and have fashioned it into their self-portrait. We present that portrait for your perusal in the following pages. Please take care to maintain and preserve this collection, for who knows when the real PAC Ten may slip into a disastrous tomorrow.

Marina N. Haan
Richard B. Hammerstrom

# CONTENTS

# Graffiti in the PAC 10

# I'd quit school, but it's the only place I can get any sleep!

*U of Washington – Bagley Hall*

The PAC Ten graffitiist leaves no illusions unturned in displaying his deep appreciation for the unique privilege of education.

*OREGON – LAWRENCE HALL*

We are the enemies of authority.
We play in the fields of freedom.

*U of Washington – Suzzallo*
*Library*

*I KNOW WHAT I LIKE, AND I LIKE WHAT I KNOW.*
*U OF WASHINGTON – ART*
*BUILDING*

**EVERYTHING YOU KNOW IS WRONG!**
*UCLA – FRANZ HALL*

I am always ready to learn, but I don't always like to be taught.
*Washington State – Holland Library*

YOU CAN'T TEACH 'EM HOW TO WRITE, BUT YOU
CAN LEARN 'EM WHAT TO SAY.
*BERKELEY – BOALDT LAW*

All this studying for what? I'll probably end up running a
pet shop?

*– below –*

Naw, come with me. I'm gonna grow strawberries and
read paperbacks, or maybe bake bread.

*– below –*

**I'll go! I'll go!**

*– below –*

**I can build fences and make real good casserole.**

*– below –*

**But can the kid tap dance?**

*USC – Doheny Library*

*NOTES FROM OFF CAMPUS:*
*HAPPINESS IS A WARM LIBRARY.*

*STANFORD – MEYER LIBRARY*

**HAVE YOU HUGGED YOUR TEXTBOOK TODAY?**

*ARIZONA STATE – SOCIAL*
*SCIENCES*

Life is too short to waste at college.

*– below –*

But it will seem too long without it.

*U of Washington – Balmer Hall*

SOMEDAY THIS WILL ALL BE WORTH IT—I HOPE.

*USC – DOHENY LIBRARY*

College is over-rated.

*– below –*

Over-sexed.

*– below –*

Well, at least over-rated. And 1 out of 2 isn't bad.

*USC – Doheny Library*

ALL WILL COME TO KNOW
COME REVELATION DAY
THE NUMBER OF THE BEAST
DIVIDES US AND SENDS US
TO QUADS WE CAN NEVER LOCATE
ON OUR OWN.

*STANFORD – MEYER LIBRARY*

It's finals time, kids. Take whites!

*U of Washington – Johnson Hall*

I NEVER HAVE MY SHIT TOGETHER FOR FINALS.

*BERKELEY – BOALDT LAW*

I think that finals are gonna do me in this time.

*U of Washington – Odegaard
Library*

It would have been better if I hadn't been born.

*Stanford – Union*

HERE I SIT ON THE JOHN NOT KNOWING WHAT MY LIFE IS ABOUT, WHERE I'M GOING OR WHY I DON'T CARE. TOMORROW SOMEONE MAY FIND A BLOODY DISPLAY OF HUMAN MISERY, AS I AM THINKING ABOUT JUMPING FROM THIS BUILDING.

*– BELOW –*

GOOD! HURRY UP AND DO IT! IF THE ONLY GRAFFITI THAT YOU CAN WRITE IS THIS SELF-INDULGENT, SELF-PITYING AND PSEUDO-EXISTENTIAL GARBAGE, LET ME KNOW AND I MAY GIVE YOU A PUSH MYSELF.

PLEASE PUT DOWN PLASTIC, THOUGH. YOU DON'T HAVE THE RIGHT TO MAKE CLEANUP HARD FOR THE GROUNDS KEEPER.

*ARIZONA STATE – ART*

*Washington State–Science*
*Area Library*

U of Arizona/Social Science

**Do you realize that you are the type of person that your good parents warned you about when you were young?**

*U of Washington – Smith Hall*

*YOU ARE A ZIT ON THE FACE OF HUMANITY!*

*UCLA – SCHOENBERG HALL*

**(BELOW PICTURE OF PENIS)**
**SEE YOURSELF AS OTHERS SEE YOU.**

*USC – SCIENCE HALL*

Your father beats off in confusion!

*Washington State – Science Area Library*

YOUR MOTHER IS LIKE A RAILROAD TRACK; SHE'S LAID ALL ACROSS THE COUNTRY.

*STANDFORD – MITCHELL HALL*

Frat rats are over-rated mice!

Fraternities and sororities appear to be experiencing an affectionate revival in the PAC Ten.

Fraternities are the outhouses of life.

GREEKS ARE PEOPLE TOO.

– BELOW –

SO ARE THE WALKING DEAD.

**Half the world is white and free.**
**The other half is SAE.**

*Oregon State – Kerr Library*


*IF YOU CAN'T GO GREEK, GO TEKE.*

*U OF WASHINGTON – GOULD*
*HALL*


**I PHELTA THI**

*– BELOW –*

**TAPPA KEGA BUD**

*ARIZONA STATE – LANGUAGE &*
*LITERATURE*


Greeks are elitist cocksuckers. Big heads, small brains.

*Washington State – Todd Hall*


FACE IT! ALL YOU SORORITY AND FRATERNITY
MEMBERS HAVE YOUR HEADS UP YOUR BUTTS, ARE
IMMATURE, PLASTIC AND SATURATED TO CAPACITY
WITH ALCOHOL.

*U OF WASHINGTON –*
*ODEGAARD LIBRARY*


**One thing about sorority women.**
**They play real good football.**

*Berkeley – Wheeler Hall*

*SORORITY GIRLS—SHORT-TERM SPERM BANKS.*
                        *USC – DOHENY LIBRARY*


**SNACK AT YOUR LOCAL SORORITY.**
**"LAY DOWN A TWENTY AND I'LL GIVE YOU PLENTY."**
                        ***USC – DOHENY LIBRARY***


Frat Rat! This is Pullman! God help you if the sun ever sets on you here.

                        *Washington State – Johnson Hall*


WHAT ARE ALL THREE GREEKS DOING IN THE MEN'S ROOM?

                        *ARIZONA STATE – ART*


**Send a Greek to war and insure your daughter's virginity.**

***– below –***

**Better yet, send a dormie to war and insure your son's virginity.**

                        ***Washington State – Todd Hall***

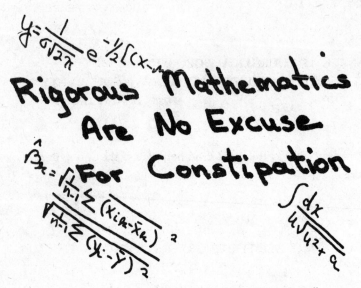

$$y = \frac{1}{\sigma\sqrt{2\pi}} e^{-\frac{1}{2}[(x-...}$$

Rigorous Mathematics
Are No Excuse
For Constipation

$$\hat{\beta}_x = \frac{\sqrt{\frac{1}{n\cdot i}\sum(x_{i\alpha}-\bar{x}_{\alpha})^2}}{\sqrt{\frac{1}{n\cdot i}\sum(y_i-\bar{y})^2}}$$

$$\int \frac{dx}{u\sqrt{u^2+a}}$$

*Oregon State – Ag Hall*

PAC Ten students can barely contain their enthusiasm for their fields of study.


WHAT'S THE DIFFERENCE BETWEEN CHEMISTRY
AND A BUCKET OF SHIT?
THE BUCKET.

*UCLA – FRANZ HALL*


**I'm flunking Chem!**

*– below –*

**So, who isn't?**

*Washington State – Fullmer Hall*

*I WILL GET AN A ON MY CHEM FINAL.*

*OREGON STATE – KERR LIBRARY*

**ABANDON ALL HOPE, YE WHO MAJOR IN CHEMISTRY.**

***WASHINGTON STATE – FULLMER HALL***

The study of entomology is driving me buggy.

*Washington State – Johnson Hall*

HIGH THERE!

*– BELOW –*

DENDROLOGY HAS SHATTERED HIS MIND.

*WASHINGTON STATE – JOHNSON HALL*

**Ontogeny recapitulates phylogeny.**

***Washington State – Sloan Hall***

*OLD BIOLOGISTS NEVER DIE, THEY JUST WRITE REVIEWS.*

*U OF OREGON – SCIENCE HALL*

BIOLOGISTS SUCK SHIT!

*– BELOW –*

HEY, THOSE SPECIAL LITTLE SHIT-SUCKING MACHINES ARE EXPENSIVE.

*U OF WASHINGTON – JOHNSON HALL*

Seeing all this makes me glad I'm a business major.

*U of Washington – Bagley Hall*
*(Biology)*

BUSINESS—BORING, LIFELESS BUSINESS.

*BERKELEY – BARROWS HALL*

What happens to people who can't get into business school?

*– below –*

They go into political science.

*– below –*

Hopefully they will become radicals and overthrow you corporate pigs and your system.

*U of Washington – Suzzallo Library*

*RELIEVE STRESS—TRANSFER TO POLITICAL SCIENCE.*
*UCLA – KINSEY HALL*

**I HATE THIS PLACE. I'M GOING BACK TO ART SCHOOL.**

*– BELOW –*

**I'VE NEVER BEEN TO ART SCHOOL, BUT IT SURE SOUNDS GOOD RIGHT NOW.**
**BERKELEY – DWINELLE HALL**

Architecture Students: Find out where your education is leading you. Demand a voice in what you are learning.
*USC – Watt Hall*

TREES ARE SIMPLY IMITATIONS OF FAN VAULTING AS DEMONSTRATED BY THE MEDIEVAL ENGLISH.
*BERKELEY – WURSTER HALL*

**Architecture sucks!**
*Arizona State – Architecture*

*ARCHITECTURE: ALL IN ALL IT'S BRICKS IN THE WALL.*
*U OF ARIZONA – ARCHITECTURE*

**BUT RIGHT NEED NOT BE WRIGHT, RIGHT?**
*ARIZONA STATE –*
*ARCHITECTURE*

**Get your rocks off in Geology!**

*UCLA – Geology*

*GEOLOGISTS ARE HARD AS A ROCK!*

*– BELOW –*

*ONLY FROM THE NECK UP.*

*UCLA – GEOLOGY*

**GEOGRAPHERS CAN RELATE TO THEIR WORLD.**

*U OF WASHINGTON – SMITH HALL*

Mathematics is the language that God used to write the Universe.

*U of Oregon – Deady Hall*

YOU CALL YOURSELVES MATHEMATICIANS? I'LL BET YOU COULDN'T TELEGRAPH FROM A HOLE IN THE GROUND.

*BERKELEY – EVANS HALL*

**Calculus is what's wrong with physics.**

*USC – Seaver Science Center*

*PHYSICS IS GOOD.*

– BELOW –

*THEN GODZILLA DRIVES AN MG.*

USC – SEAVER SCIENCE CENTER

**PHYSICS 116 IS SOPHOMORIC!**

**U OF OREGON – SCIENCE MAIN
BLOCK**

Be incomprehensible. If they can't understand, they can't
disagree.

*– below –*

A lesson all physics profs know well.

*U of Washington – Physics*

OLD PHYSICISTS DON'T DIE, THEIR PROBABILITY
DISTRIBUTIONS GO TO ZERO AS *T* GOES TO INFINITY.

U OF WASHINGTON – PHYSICS

**Willie was a scientist
But now he is no more.
What Willie thought was $H_2O$
Was $H_2SO_4$.**

**U of Washington – Smith Hall**

*CONTRARY TO WHAT THE NAME MIGHT IMPLY,
AUGER SPECTROSCOPY IS NOT THAT DULL.*

*U OF WASHINGTON – PHYSICS*

**RHO, RHO, RHO YOUR BOAT
GENTLY DOWN THE STREAM.
MERRILY, MERRILY, MERRILY,
CONTINUITY IS BUT A DREAM**

***OREGON STATE – AG HALL***

20% of engineers are space cases.
75% are a little weird.
5% are completely normal.
They're so cool you wouldn't know they're engineers.
After 18 months I've had it working with engineers.

*USC – Seaver Science Center*

TYPICAL ENGINEERING STUDENT.

*BERKELEY-WURSTER HALL*

**Engineering sex manual: In, out, repeat if necessary.**

*Oregon State – Dearborn Hall*

*IN THE BEGINNING GOD CREATED THE HARDWARE AND THE SOFTWARE.*

*– BELOW –*

*THEN THE DEVIL CREATED BUGS AND QUEUES.*

*STANFORD – CENTER FOR*
*EDUCATION & RESEARCH*

**LAW STUDENTS ARE ONE FOR THE BOOKS.**

*STANFORD – LAW*

Hard cases make bad lawyers.

*– below –*

Bad lawyers make hard cases.

*Berkeley – Boaldt Law*

Q:   HOW DO YOU BEAT A STANFORD LAWYER?
A:   TAKE HIM TO COURT.

*STANFORD – LAW*

**Become a doctor, support a lawyer.**

*Berkeley – Boaldt Law*

*BECOME AN INDUSTRIAL DESIGNER AND LEARN TO DRAW ASHTRAYS AND MICROWAVES.*

*U OF WASHINGTON – ART*

**PSUCKOLOGY!**

***UCLA – FRANZ HALL***

I like Psychology. It's the only class where I can eat lunch and take a nap.

*UCLA – Franz Hall*

HOW COME PSYCHOLOGY MAJORS ARE SO OBSESSED WITH SEX?

*– BELOW –*

BECAUSE ALL YOU ECON MAJORS NEED SOMEONE TO LOOK UP TO.

*UCLA – FRANZ HALL*

**Psychologist's Motto: If you can't dazzle them with your brilliance, baffle them with your bullshit.**

***Washington State – Johnson Tower***

*THE MAIN PROBLEM WITH THE WORLD IS THAT THERE ARE NO JOBS FOR HISTORY MAJORS.*

*BERKELEY – DWINELLE HALL*

*THIS UNIVERSITY IS A PATHETIC JOKE !!!*

*BERKELEY – BOALDT LAW*

PAC Ten graffiti subtly convey the high regard in which students hold their alma mater.

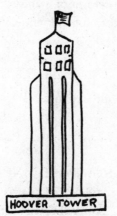

Hoover's last erection.

*Stanford – Meyer Library*

STANFORD—THE YALE OF THE WEST.

*STANFORD – UNION*

**Stanford—the Harvard of the West.**

***Stanford – Meyer Library***

*STANFORD—THE MICHIGAN OF THE WEST.*

*– BELOW –*

*GO SUCK A WOLVERINE!*

*STANFORD – UNION*

**STANFORD—THE STANFORD OF THE WEST.**

***STANFORD – DURAND HALL***

Suggestion for the reform of Stanford as an institution: Use the Inner Quad as ground zero for thermo nuclear target practice.

*– below –*

Hell, just wait for the earthquake.

*Stanford – Union*

STANFORD: AT STANFORD UNIVERSITY THEY TEACH US TO WASH OUR HANDS AFTER WE URINATE.
YALE: AT YALE, THEY TEACH US NOT TO PISS ON OUR HANDS.

*– BELOW –*

21

ILLINOIS: WE DID NOT NEED TO BE TAUGHT.

*– BELOW –*

UCLA: THEY TEACH US TO SQUAT.

*– BELOW –*

MIT: WE HAVE MACHINES TO PEE FOR US.
*STANFORD – LAW*

**How do you separate the men from the boys at Stanford? With a crowbar.**

***Berkeley – Dwinelle Hall***

*Q: WHAT'S THE DIFFERENCE BETWEEN STANFORD WOMEN AND A 747?*
*A: ABOUT TEN POUNDS.*

*STANFORD – MEYER LIBRARY*

**WHAT STANFORD WOMAN WOULD LOWER HERSELF TO BEAR CHILDREN?**

***STANFORD – MEYER LIBRARY***

Stanford's usual big game victory only indicates the inverse relationship between football and intelligence.

*Berkeley – Evans Hall*

HA! STANFORD ISN'T GOING TO THE ROSE BOWL!
*BERKELEY – WURSTER HALL*

**Stanford**
**Stanford**
**Stanford**
**Stanford**
**Fuck it!**

*Stanford – Meyer Library*


*I GOT THE U OF A BLUES.*

*U OF ARIZONA – PSYCHOLOGY*


**AFTER 5 YEARS AND 148 HOURS, I WOULD JUST LIKE TO SAY THAT COLLEGE HAS TAUGHT ME THE IMPORTANCE OF DRUGS, SEX, AND ROCK & ROLL.**

*U OF ARIZONA – MODERN LANGUAGES*


Among the market place of ideas, ASU is a discount cellar.

*Arizona State – Social Sciences*


WAZZOO WANTS YOU!

*U OF WASHINGTON – BALMER HALL*


Sometimes there is remarkable agreement of opinion.


**WSU sucks!**

*U of Washington – Odegaard Library*

*WSUCKS!*

> *WASHINGTON STATE – JOHNSON HALL*

**THE TIME HAS COME FOR THE NORTHWEST TO SECEDE FROM THE UNION. "ECOTOPIA"**

> *U OF OREGON – LAWRENCE HALL*

U of Oregon, you taught me everything from A to B.

> *U of Oregon – Prince Lucien Campbell*

OREGON—THE NATION'S BUTTOCKS.

> *U OF OREGON – CONDON HALL*

**Oregon—the tampon of the U.S.**

> ***U of Oregon – Condon Hall***

*OREGON—I'D RATHER BE IN HARLEM.*

*– BELOW –*

*WE'D RATHER HAVE YOU THERE TOO.*

> *U OF OREGON – CONDON HALL*

**OREGON—THE MORE CALIFORNIANS THE BETTER.**

*– BELOW –*

**NOT REALLY, WE ALREADY HAVE ENOUGH FRUITS AND NUTS.**

*U OF OREGON – CONDON HALL*

Happiness is a Californian leaving Washington with a New Yorker under each arm.

*U of Washington – Balmer Hall*

I AM GOING BACK TO NEW YORK CITY!

*BERKELEY – UNION*

**New York is real; the rest is done with mirrors.**

*Stanford – English*

*LA IS A WASTELAND. ASK ANYONE FROM ASHLAND, OREGON.*

*– BELOW –*

*I WAS IN ASHLAND ONCE. IT WAS CLOSED.*

*UCLA – MELNITZ HALL*

**HEY YOU! YEH, YOU, L.A.! YOU, TINSEL TOWN, GET SOME CULTURE.**

*BERKELEY – LECONTE HALL*

California is a confused state.

*Berkeley – Wheeler Hall*


ALL THAT CALIFORNIANS REALLY NEED IS A GOOD BLIZZARD SO THAT THEY CAN GET SNOWED IN AND CONTEMPLATE THEIR MINISCULE PLACE IN THIS UNIVERSE. GREETINGS FROM MINNESOTA.

*LA INTERNATIONAL AIRPORT*


**Free California from the Union!**

***UCLA – Kinsey Hall***


*FUCK ME!*

*– BELOW –*

*IF YOU ARE A UCLA STUDENT, THEY ALREADY DID.*

*UCLA – Young Hall*


**THIS TRASHY LIBRARY TYPIFIES THE ACADEMIC INFERIORITY OF USC! I HAD A CHOICE—USC OR UCLA. I CHOSE UCLA. THANK GOD! THIS PLACE IS SO RUN-DOWN! DON'T YOU HAVE ANY PRIDE IN YOURSELVES? THOSE OF YOU WITH INTELLIGENCE, JOIN US AT UCLA.**

**P.S. I WROTE THIS IN PENCIL SO THAT IT CAN BE ERASED. I AM NOT A VANDAL. JUST A CONCERNED STUDENT WITH A MESSAGE.**

***USC – DOHENY LIBRARY***

UCLA belongs in the Rose Bowl; USC in the toilet bowl.

*USC – Chemical Engineering*

WELCOME TO THE PAC 5!

*UCLA – FRANZ HALL*

**Ohio State Football isn't worth a fart!**

**UCLA – Law**

*WHY DID USC NAME THEIR FOOTBALL TEAM AFTER A BRAND OF RUBBERS?*

*UCLA – POWELL LIBRARY*

**TROJANS BURST UNDER PRESSURE!**

**USC – DOHENY LIBRARY**

I love SC song girls.

*USC – Science Center*

USC—UNIVERSITY OF SLEEPING CUNTS.

*USC – VON KLEINSMID CENTER*

**This is the only school I know where you can do your homework on what looks like a bathroom wall.**

**USC – Doheny Library**

*WORRY THAT THERE ARE PEOPLE BEING ADMITTED
TO UC-BERKELEY WHO CAN'T EVEN SPELL 'FASCISTS.'*

*BERKELEY – WURSTER HALL*

**BERKELEY—THE PLAYGROUND OF THE CONSCIENCE-
RIDDEN IDEALIST.**

*BERKELEY – UNION*

**For every activist there is an equal and opposite
reactionary.**

*Berkeley – Evans Hall*

*MOM, WHY DON'T THEY HIRE BERKELEY GRADS?*

*BERKELEY – WURSTER HALL*

**FUCKING FOR VIRGINITY IS LIKE GOING TO BERKELEY
FOR AN EDUCATION.**

*BERKELEY – WHEELER HALL*

I've spent ten years in different jails and two years in Berkeley
University.

*– below –*

That's nothing, try a week in Sacramento.

*– below –*

How about an afternoon in Lodi.

*Berkeley – Dwinelle Hall*

Given enough time, a monkey with a Flair pen would stoop to this graffiti.

*U of Oregon – Prince Lucien Campbell*

PAC Ten graffitiists occasionally pause to debate the literary merits of their art form.

*GRAFFITI IS JUVENILE!*

*UCLA – ENGINEERING*

**BATHROOM GRAFFITI IS AN ARTFORM.**

***U OF ARIZONA – MODERN LANGUAGES***

Graffiti must not mean, but be.

*U of Washington – Art Building*

THIS GRAFFITI IS CHILDISH. BE ADULT!

*– BELOW –*

THIS COUNTRY NEEDS MORE DULTS.

*UCLA – MOORE HALL*

**Graffiti are mental excrement, and so belong in bathrooms.**

*Berkeley – Giannini Hall*

*A SOPHOMORE IN PHYSICS NAMED RAFFERTY*
*CAME TO THE GENTLEMEN'S LAFFITY.*
*WHEN THE WALLS MET HIS SIGHT,*
*HE SAID, "NEWTON WAS RIGHT.*
*THIS MUST BE THE CENTER OF GRAFFITI."*

*U OF WASHINGTON –*
*ODEGAARD LIBRARY*

**WRITING ON THE WALLS MAKES ONE IMMORTAL!**

**– *BELOW* –**

**(AT LEAST UNTIL IT'S PAINTED OVER.)**

*OREGON STATE – KERR LIBRARY*

Those who write on bathroom walls always seem to rhyme without reason.

*U of Arizona – Education*

IMPRESSIVE DISPLAY OF THE INTELLIGENCE AT UCLA.

*UCLA – FRANZ HALL*

**I'm impressed by Stanford graffiti. Cal Poly still gets off on Aggie humor.**

***Stanford – Union***

*THAT'S THE BITCH ABOUT GRADUATING FROM STANFORD, YOU HAVE TO DRIVE 350 MILES TO COME BACK AND READ INFORMED GRAFFITI.*

*—UCLA BIZ SCHOOL*
*STANFORD – UNION*

**I CAN'T BELIEVE THE PISS-POOR GRAFFITI AT ASU.**

***ARIZONA STATE – EDUCATION***

The University of Minnesota has better graffiti.

*U of Washington – Padelford Hall*

I THINK IT'S TIME TO CHANGE MY TRESSIDER STALL. THESE COMMENTS ARE ALL RE-RUNS.

*STANFORD – UNION*

**This wall is in its 19th printing.**

***U of Arizona – Library***

*I PITY YOU WHOSE INTELLECT IS STIMULATED BY THE SMELL OF THIS COMPARTMENT.*

*USC – VON KLEINSMID CENTER*

**BATHROOM HUMOR: WIT AND SHIT.**

***ARIZONA STATE – ART***

I agree with all of the strange, weird, sick, perverted opinions displayed on this wall on two bases:
1.   Everyone is entitled to their opinion.
2.   I am a Democrat.

*USC – Von Kleinsmid Center*

WATCH OUT! IN JAIL THEY SAY THAT IF YOU LEAVE YOUR MARK ON THE WALL YOU WILL COME BACK.

*ARIZONA STATE – ART*

**To all girls who read stall notes but never write: I find that a lot of girls have the same problems—they are either frustrated with Stanford men or Stanford life and I know that there are a numerous amount of girls who share these frustrations but are afraid to write. I guess what I'm getting at is that you shouldn't be afraid to write on the stalls. You're not a bad person for doing so and who knows, someone might be able to help you and even better, you could help someone else. So don't just sit there—get your pens out.**

***Stanford – Meyer Library***

*COME ON NOW, THE MUSIC BUILDING SHOULD BE FILLED WITH GRAFFITI, NOT GRAFFICKY.*

*U OF ARIZONA – MUSIC*

**THIS INTELLECTUAL MASTURBATION IS THE DUBIOUS PRIVILEGED.**

*STANFORD – CENTER FOR*
*EDUCATION RESEARCH*

Sometimes I wonder if people really think in these terms.

*Berkeley – Giannini Hall*

(AFTER A LIST OF NAMES)
FOOLS' NAMES AND FOOLS' FACES ARE ALWAYS FOUND IN PUBLIC PLACES.

*WASHINGTON STATE –*
*HOLLAND LIBRARY*

Graffiti sometimes takes a therapeutic turn . . .

**I feel sorry for you. You sound really sad and angry and helpless. Try talking with someone about what's bothering you. Because it's a bad scene when you've got to vent your frustrations on a toilet stall wall—They just aren't that sympathetic.**

But not always.

*– below –*

**So leave lady. No one is asking you to stay.**

*Stanford – Meyer Library*

*PENTEL MADE THIS GRAFFITI POSSIBLE.*

– BELOW –

*BOREDOM MADE THIS GRAFFITI POSSIBLE.*

UCLA – GEOLOGY

Some schools provide their own graffiti materials as a defensive measure. Stanford Law Building, for example, provides chalkboards. This policy has still not proved completely successful.

**$6,434 PER YEAR AND YOU'VE GOTTA SUPPLY YOUR OWN CHALK!**

STANFORD – LAW BUILDING

Fine Arts 199—3 credits: Introduction to Bathroom Graffiti.

Washington State – Find Arts

PRESS-ON GRAFFITI

(USING PRESS-ON LETTERING)<br>U OF OREGON – LAWRENCE<br>HALL

**This space reserved for thoughtful graffiti.**

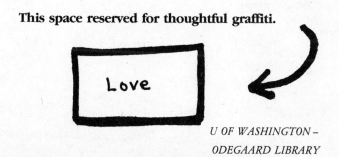

U OF WASHINGTON –<br>ODEGAARD LIBRARY

34

Graffitiists recognize not only the ephemeral nature of their art but also its toughest critic.

**JANITORS WORK AGAINST NATURE!**

*U OF WASHINGTON – ODEGAARD LIBRARY*

Wall washers, be warned!

*UCLA – Kinsey Hall*

THEY PAINT THE WALLS TO STOP MY PEN,
BUT THE SHITHOUSE POET STRIKES AGAIN.

*USC – CHEMICAL ENGINEERING*

**To the custodian: Sir, the walls are a public forum, a sacred vessel of imperishable ideas. You may wash them away, but you will never erase them.**

*Arizona State – Hayden Library*

*HI, I'M THE GUY WHO WRITES ALL OF THIS ON THE WALL. THEY PAY ME TO DO IT, TOO. REALLY! IF I DIDN'T WRITE, THE JANITORS WOULDN'T HAVE ANYTHING TO CLEAN UP, AND THEY'D ALL BE FIRED. I HELP THE ECONOMY.*

*WASHINGTON STATE – FINE ARTS*

**IF YOU DON'T LIKE THE WRITINGS ON THIS WALL,
MANAGEMENT WILL REMOVE THEM.**

*BERKELEY – DWINELLE HALL*

Janitor, clean this wall!

*– below –*

Clean it yourself, asshole!

*U of Washington – Electrical
Engineering*

SEE! THIS IS WHAT YOU GET FOR SEEKING HIGHER
TRUTHS.

*U OF WASHINGTON – PHYSICS*

*Save the whales! —*
*Hold the anchovies!*

**Berkeley – Boaldt Law**

The time-honored technique of the wry retort is raised to new heights by the PAC Ten graffitiist.

*JESUS SAVES!*

*– BELOW –*

*AT BAGHDAD SAVINGS.*

*CLASSIC ON ALL CAMPUSES*

**WHAT PRICE GLORY?**
**WHAT PRICE FREEDOM?**

*– BELOW –*

**$14.95—AVAILABLE AT WOOLCO DRUGS.**
*STANFORD – MITCHELL HALL*

Long live life!

*– below –*

Yeh, I don't like Newsweek.

*Berkeley – Dwinelle Hall*

KILL WHITEY!

*– BELOW –*

WHAT DID WHITEY FORD EVER DO TO YOU?

*U OF WASHINGTON – SMITH
HALL*

**Why are there so many smart alecks around here?**

*– below –*

**Silly, that's why they come to school. They used to be dumb alecks.**

*Oregon State – Dearborn Hall*

*SAVE SOVIET JEWS!*

– BELOW –

*WIN VALUABLE PRIZES!*

                      *CLASSIC ON ALL CAMPUSES*

**THE DISTINGUISHING CHARACTERISTIC OF MONEY IS ITS LIQUIDITY. THE MORE LIQUID SOMETHING IS, THE MORE MONEYLIKE IT IS. WHEN IT IS COMPLETELY LIQUID, IT HAS ATTAINED THE ZENITH OF MONEYNESS.**

*– BELOW –*

**TAKE OIL, FOR EXAMPLE.**

                    *U OF WASHINGTON – ODEGAARD LIBRARY*

Eternity is forever.

*– below –*

What was your first clue?

                    *Berkeley – Dwinelle Hall*

JOHN WAS HERE, CLASS OF 1981.

*– BELOW –*

TOM WAS HERE, CLASS OF WHENEVER I CAN GET ENOUGH CREDITS.

                    *WASHINGTON STATE – FULLMER HALL*

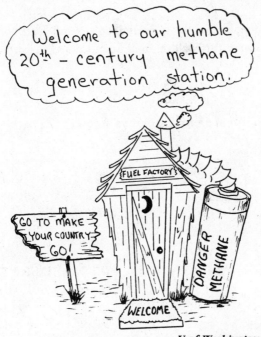

*U of Washington – Denny Hall*

The joys of the toilet are often left unsung, but PAC Ten graffitiists are not deterred by cultural taboos.

*WELCOME TO USC'S SACRED GROUNDS, OFFERING PRIVACY AND SECLUSION.*

*USC – SCIENCE CENTER*

**WELCOME TO THE ORCA SHOW, LADIES AND GENTLEMEN. WATCH ORCA SPLASH IN THE WATER.**

*U OF ARIZONA – ARCHITECTURE*

40

There is someone humming Beethoven's Ninth Symphony in the Men's stall behind this wall. Men at Stanford are weird.

*– below –*

Oh, come on! It is pretty famous, ya' know.

*– below –*

He's singing it again.

*Stanford – Meyer Library*

THIS IS YOUR RELAXATION TIME—MAXIMIZE IT.

*U OF WASHINGTON – PHYSICS*

**Really don't mind
If you sit this one out.
My turd's but a whisper,
Your deafness' a shout.**

**U of Washington – Suzzallo
Library**

Rodin's " The Stinker"

*U OF OREGON – SCIENCE II*

**DON'T JUST SIT THERE, DO SOMETHING.**

*OREGON STATE – AG HALL*

Here I sit broken hearted,
Tried to shit
But only farted.

*Classic on all campuses*

HEY, BUCKO! TAKE IT EASY. DON'T TRY TOO HARD.
IT'LL BLOW YOUR ASS OUT.

*U OF OREGON – PRINCE LUCIEN
CAMPBELL*

**Watch out! Your shit is f$_{alling}$**

$^{out}$...

**Gravity wins again!**

*Washington State – Science Area
Library*

*WARNING: ANYTHING OVER FIVE POUNDS, LOWER
WITH A ROPE.*

*BERKELEY – WURSTER HALL*

**HERE I SIT ON THE POOPER,
JUST GAVE BIRTH TO ANOTHER STATE TROOPER.**

*CLASSIC ON ALL CAMPUSES*

Here I sit, buns a flexin'
Just gave birth to another Texan.

*Classic on all campuses*


NOTICE: PLEASE FLUSH TWICE, THE COMMONS IS
FAR.

*CLASSIC ON ALL CAMPUSES*


**If you took a shit here, please bring it back, no questions
asked.**

***Washington State – Science
Library***


*ANOTHER SHITTY DAY.*

*WASHINGTON STATE – SCIENCE
AREA LIBRARY*


**WHY IS THERE SO MUCH INTEREST IN 'SHIT'?**

*– BELOW –*

**I FIND THIS WORD OFFENSIVE. WHY NOT SAY "HUMAN
WASTE?"**

*– BELOW –*

**OR POO-POO**

*– BELOW –*

**OR #2**

*– BELOW –*

**OR DUNG**

*– BELOW –*

**OR CAA-CAA**

*– BELOW –*

**OR FECES (ENDANGERED)**

*– BELOW –*

**OR DOO-DOO**

*– BELOW –*

**OR LOAF (AS IN "PINCH A LOAF")**

*– BELOW –*

**OR UNKO**

*USC – DOHENY LIBRARY*

Eat shit; 10 billion flies can't be wrong.

*Classic on all campuses*

NO MATTER WHAT ANYONE SAYS, IT BOILS DOWN TO WHAT YOU ATE LAST.

*U OF OREGON – LAWRENCE HALL*

**A foot is worth a thousand turds.**
**—Aristotle (the Greek philosopher, not shipping magnate)**

*Stanford – Center for Education*
*Research*

*BE LIKE DAD, NOT LIKE SIS,*
*LIFT THE LID BEFORE YOU PISS.*

*CLASSIC ON ALL CAMPUSES*

**THIS IS THE WONG PLACE.**

*U OF ARIZONA – EDUCATION*

Don't look up here, the joke's in your hand.

*Classic on all campuses*

THERE IS NO SUCH THING AS MORRAY EELS IN
TOILETS, IS THERE? NAH, COULDN'T BE. ARRGHH . . .

*WASHINGTON STATE – FINE*
*ARTS*

**Don't throw toothpicks in our toilet,**
**The crabs have learned to pole vault.**

*Classic on all campuses*

*BUTTERFLIES HAVE THE WINGS OF GOLD.*
*MOTHS HAVE WINGS OF FLAME.*
*TOILET CRABS HAVE NO WINGS AT ALL*
*BUT GET THERE JUST THE SAME.*

*BERKELEY – BOALDT LAW*

**ANYBODY CAN PISS ON THE FLOOR, BUT IT TAKES A MAN TO SHIT ON THE CEILING.**

*CLASSIC ON ALL CAMPUSES*

Don't throw your cigarette butts in the urinal; they're too hard to relight.

*U of Arizona – Home Ec and Business*

JUST THINK OF ALL THE BUTTS THAT HAVE BEEN HERE, WHITE BUTTS, BLACK BUTTS, BROWN BUTTS, YELLOW BUTTS, BUTTS, BUTTS, BUTTS . . . I THINK I'LL GET UP.

*U OF WASHINGTON – SMITH HALL*

**This bathroom cost me a lot; please pay as you go.**

**Rose Budd – Garden Grove, Calif.**

*THE JOB ISN'T DONE UNTIL THE PAPERWORK IS FINISHED.*

*ARIZONA STATE – LANGUAGE AND LITERATURE*

**THERE AIN'T NO COBS HERE.**

**ARIZONA STATE – ART**

We've got marble walls in this stall. Now, when do we get decent paper.

*Oregon State – Moreland Hall*

*BERKELEY – UNION*

The Pac Ten graffitiist finds the architecture and accoutrements of the bathroom stall not only inspirational but challenging.

Some celebrate the formidable task of writing in the grout crack between the tiles, using this format to greatest advantage in making their point.

**BUSINESS ADMINISTRATION STUDENTS HAVE ONE-CRACK MINDS.**

*BERKELEY – BARROWS HALL*

Crack graffiti are for people with narrow minds.

*Washington State – Sloan Hall*

CRACK DOWN ON STUDYING.

*WASHINGTON STATE –*
*KIMBRAUGH HALL*

**A B C D E F G H I J K L M N O P Q R S T U V W X Y Z**
*UCLA – Kinsey Hall*

*(IN VARIOUS ADJACENT CRACKS)*
*A CRACK UP*
*BEND OVER AND CRACK A SMILE*
*ANIMAL CRACKERS*
*THAT WAS A STUPID CRACK*
*YES, BY CRACKY*
*A CRACKDOWN*

*U OF WASHINGTON – SMITH*
*HALL*

The ever-present roll of toilet paper is labeled with new insights.

**TO EACH ACCORDING TO HIS NEED.**
*U OF WASHINGTON – LOEW HALL*

ASU diploma

*Arizona State – Language and*
*Literature*

FREE DAILY TROJAN. TAKE ONE.

*USC – WATT HALL*

**Illegal alien certification papers.**

*U of Arizona – Psychology*

*B.S. IN CHEMISTRY*

*U OF ARIZONA – PSYCHOLOGY*

**IRANIAN FLAGS**

***UCLA – YOUNG HALL***

Ayatoilet paper

*Stanford – Union*

PLEASE RECORD ALL DEPOSITS MADE AFTER 3:00 PM
ON SHEETS PROVIDED.

*U OF OREGON – SCIENCE II*

**Official 1980 Summer Olympics boycott paper.**

***Arizona State – Art***

But nothing is more gratifying a subject to PAC Ten graffitiists than that peculiarly West Coast phenomenon—the disposable toilet-seat-cover dispenser. Only the PAC Ten graffitiist has managed to capture its true nature.

*ASS GASKETS!*

*L.A. INTERNATIONAL AIRPORT*

49

**POLISH TONGUE DEPRESSORS**
**SOVIET TOILET PAPER**
**OPEN ME FIRST**
**SALT II TREATIES. SIGN ONE.**

*OREGON STATE – MILAN HALL*

Iranian life preservers

*Oregon State – Kerr Library*

FREE COWBOY HATS

*U OF WASHINGTON – SMITH HALL*

**Life jackets**

*Oregon State – Withycombe Hall*

*KING KONG'S WEDDING RING*

*OREGON STATE – MILAN HALL*

**MEXICAN T-SHIRTS**

*OREGON STATE – WENIGER HALL.*

Frat bibs!

*Oregon State – Kerr Library*

DON'T FORGET YOUR FREE SOUVENIR IRANIAN
PLACE MAT.

*OREGON STATE – AG HALL*

**Reagan thinking cap**
**Carter-Mondale sore loser awards**

*Oregon State – Milan Hall*


*OUR SUBSIDY OF THE PAPER INDUSTRY*

*WASHINGTON STATE –*
*ADMINISTRATION*


**IS THIS APPROPRIATE TECHNOLOGY?**

***OREGON STATE – WENIGER HALL***


A product of the wasteful Capitalistic society.

*– below –*

Right on! Only the Party leaders should have these.

*Oregon State – Bexell Hall*


Actually, no part of this stimulating environment escapes the graffitiist's attention . . .


*(WRITTEN ON A MIRROR)* ! ꟼ⅃ƎH

*UCLA – PARKING RAMP 3*


**(pointing to a depiction of a penis)**
**All in all, it's just another prick in the wall**

***Washington State – Science Area***
***Library***

# Nothing wrong with
# RAW SEX

*U OF WASHINGTON – MUSIC*

Intimate relationships are treated with appropriate sensitivity.

$$S(e)^x = F(u)^n + VD$$

*ARIZONA STATE – PHYSICAL SCIENCE*

HOW DO YOU SPELL RELIEF? S-E-X

*WASHINGTON STATE – HOLLAND LIBRARY*

**Why don't we all fuck like animals until the next new moon.**

*U of Washington – Art Building*

*THINK BIG, FUCK AN ELEPHANT.*

*U OF ARIZONA – MODERN*
*LANGUAGES*

**LET'S ALL HAVE SEX WITH DINOSAURS.**

**U OF WASHINGTON – DENNY**
**HALL**

Support National Sex Week—give 'til it hurts!

*UCLA – Dodd Hall*

WHEN THEY LAY ME IN MY GRAVE,
NO PUSSY WILL I CRAVE
BUT ON MY TOMBSTONE WILL BE SEEN,
"HERE LIES THE BONES OF A FUCKING MACHINE."

*U OF WASHINGTON –*
*ODEGAARD LIBRARY*

**Smorgas Borgasm!**

*U of Washington – Padelford Hall*

*CANCER IS CAUSED BY SEXUAL STARVATION.*

*BERKELEY – BIRGE HALL*

**REMEMBER THE FIRST TIME YOU GOT INTO HEAVY PETTING?**

*– BELOW –*

**THE CLOSEST I EVER GOT TO HEAVY PETTING WAS A TWO HUNDRED POUND ST. BERNARD I HAD AS A KID.**

*U OF ARIZONA – PHYSICS*

Big red tigers may bite, but a little pussy never hurt anyone.

*Washington State – Kimbraugh Music*

GOT THE SUMMER HORNIES?

*WASHINGTON STATE – SCIENCE AREA LIBRARY*

**Honk if you're horny.**

*Arizona State – Art*

*ALICE HAS A HARD TIME BEING TRUE; SHE'S JUST HORNY, AND THERE'S NOTHING SHE CAN DO.*

*USC – MUDD HALL OF PHILOSOPHY*

**SHE OFFERED HER HONOR.
I HONORED HER OFFER.
SO, ALL NIGHT LONG IT WAS 'ON HER' AND 'OFF HER'.**

*CLASSIC ON ALL CAMPUSES*

Help fight against a cure for nymphomania.

*U of Arizona – Old Psychology*

A BEARDED CLAM!

*WASHINGTON STATE – SCIENCE*
*AREA LIBRARY*

**Roll her in dough and look for the wet spot.**

**Washington State – Fine Arts**

*SMILE IF IT GOT A BIT STICKY LAST NIGHT.*

*USC – DOHENY LIBRARY*

**WHEN IN DOUBT,**
**WHIP IT OUT,**
**AND MAKE HER SHOUT.**

**WASHINGTON STATE – JOHNSON**
**HALL**

b4i4q $\frac{ru,}{18}$ uqt ?

*Classic on all campuses*

OH, OH, IT'S THAT TIME OF YEAR AGAIN; SOMEONE
AIN'T GETTIN' IT.

*U OF ARIZONA – ARCHITECTURE*

**Nothing matters.**

*– below –*

**Sex does, sometimes.**

**U of Arizona – Psychology**

*SEX IS MUSICAL AND VICE VERSA.*

*BERKELEY – MORRISON HALL*

**LET'S ALL GET INTO S & M.**

*U OF ARIZONA – MODERN
LANGUAGES*

Urine fetishes can be messy.

*Oregon State – Ag Hall*

I'M INTO SEX ART.

*USC – WATT HALL*

**What, pray tell, is a flying fuck?**

*USC – Von Kleinsmid Center*

*IF YOUR BALLS WERE IN YOUR EARS, YOU COULD HEAR
YOURSELF COMING.*

*U OF ARIZONA – MODERN
LANGUAGES*

**POLYGAMY IS FUN, BUT DANGEROUS. USE CAUTION!**

*U OF WASHINGTON – ODEGAARD
LIBRARY*

The Phallic Objects Rule!

*Berkeley – Union*

THERE ONCE WAS A MAN FROM EUGENE
WHO BUILT A SEX MACHINE.
CONCAVE OR CONVEX,
WORKED FOR EITHER SEX,
BUT OH WHAT A BASTARD TO CLEAN.

*OREGON STATE – MILAN HALL*

**Born on a mountain, I live in a cave.**
**Pot and pussy are all that I crave.**

***U of Arizona – Modern Languages***

*I'M A SUCKER FOR A NICE SET OF TITS.*

*U OF WASHINGTON – MUSIC
BUILDING*

**VIRGINITY IS AN UNSOCIAL DISEASE.**

***BERKELEY – DWINELLE HALL***

Screw for sanity!

*Arizona State – Art*

VIRGINITY—THE WORTHLESS VIRTUE.

*U OF ARIZONA – UNIVERSITY
LIBRARY*

**Chastity begins at home.**

***U of Washington – Music Building***

*INCEST IS BEST.*

*USC – DOHENY LIBRARY*

Practice makes perverts!

*BERKELEY – EVANS HALL*

Pac Ten students do not always make friends easily.

Don't knock masturbation. At least it's sex with someone you love.

*U of Arizona – Architecture*

MASTURBATION IS THE ONLY ANSWER.

*– BELOW –*

TO THE INFLATION PROBLEM.

*U OF WASHINGTON –*
*ARCHITECTURE*

**Masturbation is copulation without representation.**

*U of Arizona – Education*

*SEX IS LIKE BRIDGE—IF YOU HAVE A GOOD HAND, YOU MIGHT AS WELL GO IT ALONE.*

*WASHINGTON STATE – FINE ARTS*

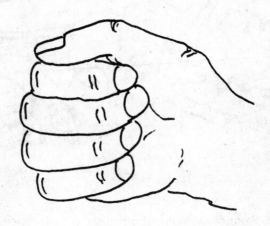

**WHAT'S THIS?**

*– BELOW –*

**BEATS ME.**

*U OF ARIZONA – PHYSICS*

Hurray for masturbation!

*– below –*

Choke your chicken!

*USC – Watt Hall*

I SAY, OLD CHAP, ARE YOU HAVING ONE OFF THE
WRIST?

*– BELOW –*

I.E., CRAMPING YOUR CROTCH

*– BELOW –*

WHIPPING YOUR LIZARD

*– BELOW –*

WHITTLING YOUR WEED

*– BELOW –*

SLAMMING YOUR HAM

*– BELOW –*

POKING YOUR POLE

*– BELOW –*

TRIMMING YOUR TREE

*– BELOW –*

NUKING YOUR WHALE

*– BELOW –*

FLOGGING YOUR DOLPHIN

*– BELOW –*

UNCORKING YOUR FLASK

*STANFORD – MITCHELL HALL*

**Men who masturbate lose their memories and can't even remember their ... ah ... er ...**

***Washington State – Johnson Tower***

*Geographers do it with*

## PRECISION!!!

*U OF ARIZONA – BUSINESS &*
*PUBLIC ADMINISTRATION*

It appears that everyone in the PAC Ten is doing "it," which leaves little doubt as to what "it" is.

**GEOGRAPHERS DO IT ALL OVER THE WORLD.**

***U OF ARIZONA – BUSINESS &***
***PUBLIC ADMINISTRATION***

Lawyers do it in their briefs.

*Berkeley – Boaldt Law*

BANKERS DO IT WITH MORE INTEREST.

*– BELOW –*

AND THERE ARE NO PENALTIES FOR EARLY WITHDRAWAL.

*WASHINGTON STATE – SCIENCE AREA LIBRARY*

**Chemists do it with SP³ hybrid bonds.**

***Oregon State – Weniger Hall***

*SCREW A TEACHER; THEY MAKE YOU GET IT RIGHT.*
*U OF ARIZONA – EDUCATION*

**MICROBIOLOGISTS DO IT IN HIGH POWER.**

***U OF ARIZONA – PSYCHOLOGY***

Ayatollahs do it religiously.

*Washington State – Science Area Library*

SKIERS GO DOWN FASTER.

*WASHINGTON STATE – SCIENCE AREA LIBRARY*

**Marines do it on the beaches, and we don't pull out until ordered by the President.**

***U of Arizona – Modern Languages***

*COWBOYS MAKE BETTER LOVERS!*

– BELOW –

*TRUE, ASK ANY COW.*

> *ARIZONA STATE – LANGUAGE &*
> *LITERATURE*

**DO IT WITH AN ARCHITECT!**

*– BELOW –*

**DO WHAT WITH AN ARCHITECT?**

*– BELOW –*

**IF YOU HAVE TO ASK, YOU COULDN'T DO IT.**

> ***ARIZONA STATE –***
> ***ARCHITECTURE***

Female architects do it with T-squares.

> *U of Arizona – Architecture*

MA BELL DOES IT LONG DISTANCE.

*– BELOW –*

WATERSKIERS STAY UP LONGER.

*– BELOW –*

64

SWIMMERS HAVE BETTER STROKES. (ESPECIALLY BREAST-STROKERS.)

*– BELOW –*

COOKS DO IT WITH SPICE AND EVERYTHING NICE.

*– BELOW –*

TEACHERS DO IT WITH CLASS.

*– BELOW –*

HUNTER-JUMPERS DO IT WITH FOXES. TALLY-HO!

*– BELOW –*

PHOTOGRAPHERS DO IT IN THE DARK. (DARKROOM, GET THE PICTURE?)

*– BELOW –*

FISHERMEN DO IT WHERE IT'S WET.

*– BELOW –*

PILOTS KEEP IT UP LONGER.

*– BELOW –*

DEBATERS DO IT ORALLY.

*– BELOW –*

COWBOYS STAY MOUNTED LONGER.

*– BELOW –*

SWIMMERS WILL CRAWL TO DO IT.

*– BELOW –*

DIVERS DO IT DEEPER, AND HAVE A SMOOTHER ENTRY.

*– BELOW –*

SURFERS RIDE IT ALL THE WAY.

*– BELOW –*

LAMBDA CHI'S DO IT WITH EACH OTHER.

*– BELOW –*

LAMBDA CHI'S DON'T KNOW HOW

*– BELOW –*

MOTO-CROSSERS DO IT WITH A TWO-STROKE.

*– BELOW –*

TREE MEN FIND BETTER CROTCHES.

*– BELOW –*

ENDURO RIDERS DO IT LONGER.

*– BELOW –*

TENNIS PLAYERS HAVE MADE IT A RACKET.

*– BELOW –*

PHYSICISTS DO IT WITH TORQUE.

*– BELOW –*

SAILORS DO IT IN THE SHEETS.

*– BELOW –*

CARPENTERS HAVE BETTER TOOLS.

*– BELOW –*

PLUMBERS DO IT WITH BIGGER PIPES.

*– BELOW –*

PROCTOLOGISTS DO IT BASS ACKWARDS.

*– BELOW –*

DEAF MUTES DO IT WITH THEIR FINGERS.

*– BELOW –*

AUSTRALIANS DO IT WITH MORE BOUNCE.

*– BELOW –*

FIREMEN DO IT WITH THEIR HOSES.

*– BELOW –*

TENNIS PLAYERS DO IT WITH LUV.

*– BELOW –*

RACE DRIVERS DO IT WHEN THEY SHIFT THEIR STICKS.

*– BELOW –*

KAMAKAZIS DO IT ONCE.

*– BELOW –*

BILLY CARTER DOES IT WITH LIBYA.

*– BELOW –*

POLITICIANS DO IT WITH:
1) COMMITTEES
2) OUR TAXES

*– BELOW –*

OREGON DUCKS DO IT BEST!

*U OF WASHINGTON –*
*ODEGAARD LIBRARY.*

*Lipstick on your dipstick?*

*U of Oregon – Science II*

PAC Ten students recognize the importance of communications in our modern world and devote considerable time to the development of appropriate oral skills.

*TELL HER TO GO DOWN.*

*WASHINGTON STATE –*
*KIMBRAUGH HALL*

**HEAD—THE FIRST ORAL CONTRACEPTIVE.**

*WASHINGTON STATE – JOHNSON*
*TOWER*

If girls are made of sugar and spice, why do they smell like tuna fish?

*Washington State – Fullmer Hall*

RIDE THE TIDE WITH TUNA.

*U OF WASHINGTON – BALMER*
*HALL*

**Do a mouse a favor—eat a pussy!**

*USC – Doheny Library*

*SAVE A FOREST, EAT A BEAVER.*

*– BELOW –*

*BETTER YET, EAT A FORESTRY STUDENT.*

*OREGON STATE – WITHYCOMBE*
*HALL*

$\sqrt{69}$ = **ATE SOMETHING**

*U OF ARIZONA – PSYCHOLOGY*

On a diet? Eat a pussy!

*UCLA – Franz Hall*

IF GOD HADN'T MEANT FOR MAN TO EAT PUSSY,
WHY DID HE MAKE IT LOOK LIKE A TACO?

*WASHINGTON STATE –*
*FULLMER HALL*

**Sit on my face and be heavy.**

*Washington State – Fullmer Hall*

*BERKELEY – UNION*

PAC Ten graffitiists have little difficulty in pinpointing priorities.

**Sing we for love and idleness—nothing else is worth the having.**

*Berkeley – LeConte Hall*

*LOVE IS THE ANSWER.*

*U OF ARIZONA – ART*

**LOVE IS A NEVER-ENDING SMILE.**

*WASHINGTON STATE – SCIENCE*
*AREA LIBRARY*

There is no such thing as love, only like and want.

*U of Oregon – Prince Lucien Campbell*

For those who love money, time is money.
For those who love, time is eternal.

*U of Arizona – Modern Languages*


REMEMBER—THE LOVE YOU TAKE IS EQUAL TO THE LOVE YOU MAKE.

*UCLA – GEOLOGY*


**Ain't love like Russian roulette?**

**U of Washington – College Inn Café**


*HELP! I'M IN LOVE AND I'M HEADIN' DOWN A ONE-WAY STREET.*

*USC – CHEMICAL ENGINEERING*


**I LOVE MAGGIE!**

**BERKELEY – UNION**


Nobody loves her like I love her.

*U of Arizona – Old Psychology*


SWEET AL LOVES YOU!

*WASHINGTON STATE – THOMPSON HALL*


**Robert Redford—I love you.**

**USC – Doheny Library**

*RITA IS LOVE!*

– BELOW –

*HAPPY ARE YOU TO KNOW HER THEN, WHETHER SHE IS YOURS OR NOT.*

*STANFORD – UNION*

**ARE WOMEN REALLY WORTH ALL THE TROUBLE?**

***U OF WASHINGTON – SUZZALLO LIBRARY***

Never saw a stump-broke horse as good as a woman.

*Arizona State – Art*

ONE GOOD THING ABOUT HOT WEATHER, YOU GET TO SEE A LOT MORE CLEAVAGE AND THIGHS.

*BERKELEY – WHEELER HALL*

**Blondes! Brunettes! Redheads!**

***Berkeley – Evans Hall***

*THE BEST WOMAN IS ONE OF NEGOTIABLE VIRTUE.*

– BELOW –

*OR NEGLIGIBLE VIRTUE.*

*USC – DOHENY LIBRARY*

73

**WOMEN SHOULD BE OBSCENE AND NOT HEARD.**
*ARIZONA STATE – ART*


Love, rain on me.

*– below –*

Love can make it rain.

*Oregon State – Ag Hall*


BE LOVED!

*– BELOW –*

I'M TRYING, BUT THEY JUST DON'T SEEM TO UNDERSTAND.

*USC – DOHENY LIBRARY*


**Men are fools because they continue to let women use sex to manipulate them.**

*U of Washington – Odegaard Library*


*I SAY FUCK THE MEN YOU DON'T CARE ABOUT AND HOLD OFF WITH THE ONES YOU DO CARE ABOUT, SO YOU CAN KEEP THE LATTER IN PERSPECTIVE.*

*BERKELEY – DWINELLE*

*Berkeley – Evans Hall*

Since the frisbee is no longer the novelty that it once was, students have turned their attention to a new toy.

*NUKE POLI SCI MAJORS!*

> *U OF WASHINGTON – SMITH*
> *HALL*

**NUKE THE GIFT OF THE CLASS OF '29!**

> ***BERKELEY – DWINELLE HALL***

Nuke the one-legged lesbian mothers!

> *U of Washington – Smith Hall*

NUKE THE FLAG-WAVERS!

*BERKELEY – DWINELLE HALL*

**I'm gonna say this just once ... nuke the Thetas now!**
**U of Washington – Balmer Hall**

*NUKE OFF BERKELEY!*

– BELOW –

*NUKE ELLINGTON!*

– BELOW –

*NUKE OF EARL!*

*BERKELEY – DWINELLE HALL*

**NUKE THE SHAH OF ANDORRA; NO ONE WOULD MISS HIM.**

**U OF WASHINGTON – COLLEGE INN CAFÉ**

Nuke nookie!

*– below –*

No! For God's sake, don't nook nookie!

*Berkeley – Wurster Hall*

NUKE THE DORMS!

*WASHINGTON STATE –*
*FULLMER HALL*

**Nuke the whales!**

*– below –*

**Inhumane, insensitive and completely separated from the reality of global ecology. Your typical physics or engineering student.**

*– below –*

**If it weren't for physicists and engineers the airheads in Social Science wouldn't know there was a 'global ecology' to worry about.**

*U of Washington – Johnson Hall*

*SAVE THE ANIMALS—EXPERIMENT WITH HUMANS!*
*U OF WASHINGTON –*
*ODEGAARD LIBRARY*

**IT CAN'T HAPPEN HERE.**

*OREGON STATE – WALDO HALL*

Whuke the nales!

*U of Washington – Denny Hall*

NUKE MR. ROGERS!

**I nuke Reagan.**
**You nuke Reagan.**
**He/she/it nukes Reagan.**

**They nuke Reagan.**
**You (pl) nuke Reagan.**
**We all should nuke
Reagan.**

***Berkeley – Dwinelle Hall***

*NUKE THE POPE!*

– BELOW –

*BAPTIZE THE BOMB!*

*BERKELEY – GIANNINI HALL*

**NUKE AMERICA SO THAT WE CAN START OVER.**

*– BELOW –*

**PAINT THIS WALL SO THAT WE CAN START OVER.**
***STANFORD – UNION***

Nuke the world, put humanity out of its misery.

*Berkeley – Dwinelle Hall*

78

– BELOW –

NO, THE BEGINNING OF A NEW REALITY.

*OREGON STATE – KERR LIBRARY*

**Reality is an artifact.**

***Berkeley – Life Sciences***

*YOU MAKE YOUR OWN REALITY. RIGHT NOW I'M TRYING TO GET RID OF MINE.*

*STANFORD – UNION*

# Couldn't **GOD** talk to **ALLAH** and settle this thing with Iran?

*UCLA – KINSEY HALL*

The drama of the Iranian crisis was played out on the walls of the PAC Ten.

Let's turn Iran into an oil slick!!!

*Berkeley – Doe Library*

BLOW IRAN OFF THE FACE OF THE EARTH!

*– BELOW –*

UNTIL IT GLOWS WOULD BE SUFFICIENT.

*USC – CHEMICAL ENGINEERING*

IRANIANS ARE CHILDREN PLAYING WITH MATCHES
IN A WOODSHED.

*U OF WASHINGTON – BALMER
HALL*

**Hey, you know what? Iranians fall in love and have babies!
I swear to God!**

**U of Arizona – Biological Science
East**

*AND THAT'S THE WAY IT IS ON THIS, THE 391ST DAY
OF CAPTIVITY FOR THOSE 52 AMERICAN HOSTAGES.*

*U OF WASHINGTON – SUZZALLO
LIBRARY*

**I JUST HEARD—THEY'RE FREE! FANTASTIC!**

***ARIZONA STATE – ART***

Here's to the Algerians!

*U of Oregon – Condon Hall*

God is a Marxist,
and the Devil
is a Capitalist.

(Just so we have
everything in black & white.)

U OF WASHINGTON – GOULD
HALL

Most ideological discussions in the PAC Ten will benefit from this clarification of terms.

**Communism is foolish idealism because of Man's greed.**

*Berkeley – Evans Hall*

*COMMUNISM OPPRESSES EVERYONE EQUALLY.*

*BERKELEY – HAVILAND HALL*

**LONG LIVE RUSSIAN EXPANSIONISM!**

*– BELOW –*

**HOPEFULLY THEY WILL NOT EXPAND AS A NATION, BUT AS INDIVIDUALS.**

*UCLA – KINSEY HALL*

Halt Communist imperialism; save humanity!

*– below –*

Halt humanity, save Communist imperialism!

*U of Washington – Odegaard Library*

CAPITALISM AND COMMUNISM ARE THE FLIP SIDE OF THE SAME COIN.

*BERKELEY – UNION*

**Let's join the Russians and rule the world.**

**UCLA – Kinsey Hall**

*FIGHT IMPERIALISM, NOT ITS WARS!*
*DOWN WITH US – USSR WAR MOVES!*

*UCLA – NORTH CAMPUS*
*STUDENT CENTER*

**IT IS NOT THE CASE THAT WE CAN FIGHT A NUCLEAR WAR AND WIN.**

**USC – MUDD HALL OF PHILOSOPHY**

**RESIST REGISTRATION!**

*– BELOW –*

**WELCOME THE FRATERNAL SOVIET TROOPS. BUT SAVE
YOUR LEVIS, THEY'LL BE WORTH RUBLES.**

*STANFORD – UNION*


80's—'Not me' decade.
90's—'No one' decade.

*Stanford – Union*


A GOOD DRAFT KEEPS THE HOME FIRES BURNING
BRIGHTLY.

*U OF OREGON – SCIENCE MAIN
BLOCK*


**If we don't stop them is S.E. Asia now, we will have to
fight them in L.A. later.**

*– below –*

**Let them have L.A.**

*U of Oregon – Science II*


*WILL YOU JOIN ME IN SMASHING THE SOVIET
UNION?—AMERICAN CAESER*

*USC – VON KLEINSMID CENTER*

**AMERICA LOVES A WINNER.**

*USC – VON KLEINSMID CENTER*

The world needs universalism, not patriotism.

*Stanford – Mitchell Hall*

THE DEGREE OF CIVILIZATION MAY BE MEASURED BY THE DEGREE TO WHICH CO-OPERATIVE INTELLIGENCE REPLACES BRUTE FORCE.

*USC – WILSON STUDENT UNION*

**Indeed, I tremble for my country when I reflect that God is just.**

***Berkeley – Dwinelle Hall***

*CAPITAL PUNISHMENT MEANS THAT THOSE WITHOUT THE CAPITAL GET THE PUNISHMENT.*

*U OF WASHINGTON – DENNY HALL*

**WHEN SHIT BECOMES OF VALUE, POOR PEOPLE WILL BE BORN WITHOUT ASSHOLES.**

***WASHINGTON STATE – FINE ARTS***

Welfare slowly but surely cripples the pride of those that receive it.

*– below –*

Why should people on welfare live their lives on an equal par with those middle-class people who support them?

*Berkeley – Wheeler Hall*


## FREE ENTERPRISE WORKS FOR THOSE WITH THE ENTERPRISES.

*U OF OREGON – PRINCE LUCIEN CAMPBELL*


**Up the ass of the ruling class!**

***Stanford – Union***


*KILL THE RICH!*

*ARIZONA STATE – ART*


**BULLY BOYS! WE KILL RICH KIDS!**

***UCLA – PARKING RAMP 3***


Die bourgeois nerds!

*– below –*

Proletarian nerds, ignore this message.

*UCLA – Melnitz Hall*


## ALL AMERICAN BANKS ARE ROBBERS.

*USC – VON KLEINSMID CENTER*

**CARS EQUAL CANCER! DRIVE TO YOUR DEATH, YOU DECADENT FOOLS!**

*– BELOW –*

**RIGHT ON! HOOFERS OF THE UNIVERSE, UNITE!**

*U OF WASHINGTON – MORE HALL*

Africa for Afrikaaners!

*Berkeley – Dwinelle Hall*

BETTER ACTIVE TODAY THAN RADIOACTIVE TOMORROW.

*STANFORD – MEYER LIBRARY*

**To split the simple atom**
**all Mankind was intent.**
**Now any day the atom**
**may return the compliment.**

**USC – Doheny Library**

*NUCLEAR INVESTMENT, POINT OF NO RETURN.*
*BERKELEY – BARROWS HALL*

**GO SOLAR! NO NUKES!**

*– BELOW –*

**NO ENERGY!**

*U OF WASHINGTON –*
*COMMUNICATIONS*

Nuclear power is safer than you think. Don't be brain-washed by Ralph Nader and the 'Small is Beautiful' people.

*U of Washington – bus stop*

FEED JANE FONDA TO THE WHALES.

*STANFORD – MEYER LIBRARY*

**Coal (alternative to nuclear = cancer & greenhouse effect (200°)**

*UCLA – Franz Hall*

*RISK NUCLEAR DEATH FOR OIL PROFITS? IT'S MEETING TIME IN JONESTOWN.*

*SAN FRANCISCO – PHONE*
*BOOTH, CALIFORNIA STREET*

**OPEN A NUCLEAR WASTE DUMP ON 1600 PENNSYLVANIA AVENUE.**

*BERKELEY – GIANNINI HALL*

Why worry about the bomb? With super VD we can all fuck ourselves to death.

*Washington State – Fullmer Hall*

PICK YOUR NOSE AND FORGET ABOUT NUCLEAR HOLOCAUST LIKE EVERYONE ELSE.

*BERKELEY – GIANNINI HALL*

# Politics is

## poopadoodle !!!

*Berkeley – Dwinelle Hall*

PAC Ten graffitiists display extraordinary insight into the nature of the American political system.

*DON'T VOTE, IT ONLY ENCOURAGES THEM.*
*U OF ARIZONA – MODERN*
*LANGUAGES*

**THE TROUBLE WITH GOVERNMENT IS THAT ALL THE CIVIL SERVANTS THINK THAT THEY ARE CIVIL MASTERS.**
*BERKELEY – EVANS HALL*

Question: What do political parties and prophylactives have in common?

Answer: Both stand for inflation, halt productivity, cover up a bunch of pricks, and give you a false sense of security while you are being fucked.

*Berkeley – Wurster Hall*


IF CON IS THE OPPOSITE OF PRO, WHAT IS THE OPPOSITE OF PROGRESS?

*CLASSIC ON ALL CAMPUSES*


**Vote Democratic and keep crime in the Congress where it belongs.**

*Berkeley – Wheeler Hall*


*NIXON, NOW MORE THAN EVER.*

*U OF WASHINGTON – SUZZALLO LIBRARY*


**ABC . . . ANYTHING BUT CARTER.**

*U OF ARIZONA – PSYCHOLOGY*


Dump Carter!

*– below –*

Can't, too busy dumping a Reagan.

*Berkeley – Union*

REAGAN IS VILE SCUM!

*WASHINGTON STATE – TODD*
*HALL*

**Ronald Reagan is a Portland laugher.**

*U of Washington – Odegaard*
*Library*

*RONALD REAGAN SHOOK MY HAND HERE.*

*ARIZONA STATE – ART*

**FOR TOO LONG A BAD FUCK HAS BEEN OVERRATED AND A GOOD SHIT UNDERRATED.**

*– BELOW –*

**BUT FINALLY REAGAN, A GOOD SHIT, HAS BEEN APPRECIATED.**

*U OF WASHINGTON – SUZZALLO*
*LIBRARY*

*WELL, YOU LIBERAL SLIME, HOW DOES IT FEEL TO BE TOTALLY REJECTED? YEH, REAGAN!*

*U OF ARIZONA – PSYCHOLOGY*

**"CAN ONE BE EXCESSIVELY MODERATE?" ASKED PERIPHENES.**
**"WELL, ONE CAN BE EXCESSIVELY MEDIOCRE," ANSWERED THE 1980 ELECTORATE.**

*BERKELEY – BOALDT LAW*

After all these years we finally have the Ray-gun.

*U of Arizona – Aeronautics*

RONALD REAGAN'S ADMINISTRATION WILL MEAN GOOD TIMES FOR CORPORATE AMERICA.

*– BELOW –*

SO WHAT? WHERE WOULD STANFORD BE WITHOUT THE RAILROADS?

*STANFORD – MITCHELL HALL*

**Berkeley beware! Reagan hates us as much as we hate him.**

***Berkeley – Wurster Hall***

*I'M GOING TO MAJOR IN THEATER SO THAT I CAN GROW UP TO BE PRESIDENT.*

*U OF WASHINGTON – SUZZALLO LIBRARY*

**RONNIE'S ROBOTS.**

***SAN FRANCISCO – NORTH BEACH AREA STREET***

If you voted for Reagan you can't shit here; your asshole's in Washington.

*Berkeley – Wheeler Hall*

REAGAN SAYS DO YOUR PART AGAINST
POLLUTION—CHOP DOWN A TREE.

*STANFORD – LAW*

**Stamp out dope—impeach Reagan.**

**U of Washington – Suzzallo**
**Library**

*IT USED TO BE 'GET THE GOVERNMENT OFF THE*
*BACKS OF THE AMERICAN PEOPLE.' NOW IT IS 'GET THE*
*PRESS OFF THE BACKS OF THE AMERICAN GOVERNMENT.'*

*WASHINGTON STATE – FINE*
*ARTS*

Down with political graffiti! Up with sex!

*U of Arizona – Pshychology*

SEX AND POLITICS!
SEX AND POLITICS!
IS THAT ALL THERE IS IN BATHROOM STALLS???

*STANFORD – ENGLISH*

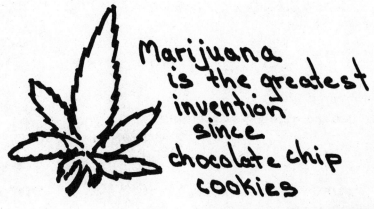

*U of Arizona – Biological Sciences*
*East*

The nature of snacks in the PAC Ten has changed in recent years.

*HIPPIE: ONE WHO LEAVES NO TURN UNSTONED.*

*U OF WASHINGTON – KANE*
*HALL*

**I WANNA BE SEDATED**

*– BELOW –*

**YOU ARE.**

*BERKELEY – UNION*

I am sedated!

*U of Washington – College Inn Café*


NO ONE KNEW, NOT EVEN HIM, THE PROBLEMS HE WOULD FIND THE DAY HE BEGAN THE JOURNEY DEEP INTO HIS MIND.

*WASHINGTON STATE – SCIENCE HALL*


**Beat the system; grow your own.**

**U of Washington – Kane Hall**


*WHEN YOU'RE IN TROUBLE,*
*WHEN YOU'RE IN DOUBT,*
*STRIKE UP A JOINT*
*AND MELLOW OUT.*

*BERKELEY – DWINELLE HALL*


**TRY PEYOTE; IT'S EYE-OPENING.**

**USC – CHEMICAL ENGINEERING**


Reality is the result of severe mescaline deficiency.

*Berkeley – Evans Hall*


REALITY IS FOR PEOPLE WHO CAN'T HANDLE DRUGS.

*– BELOW –*

CLICHÉS ARE FOR PEOPLE WHO CAN'T HANDLE CREATIVITY.

*U OF WASHINGTON – BAGLEY HALL*


**LDS consumes 47 times its weight in reality.**

***Classic on all campuses***


*LSD—CHEAPER THAN A LOBOTOMY.*

*– BELOW –*

*AND POSSIBLY JUST AS PERMANENT.*

*OREGON STATE – MILAN HALL*


**EAT ACID FOR THE END OF ALL REALITY.**

***OREGON STATE – KERR LIBRARY***


Drop acid.

*– below –*

Don't drop it; take it pass/fail.

*Arizona State – Life Sciences*


DRUGS ARE A CRUTCH!

*– BELOW –*

LIFE IS BROKEN LEG.

*USC – WATT HALL*

**Reality is a state caused by lack of drugs.**

*– below –*

**Reality is not a proper name.**

*– below –*

**Reality is an organization through which one buys property.**

*– below –*

**Mushrooms let you see reality from the outside.**

***Stanford – Center for Education Research***

*EAT 'SHROOMS!*

*OREGON STATE – KERR LIBRARY*

**MUNCH MAGIC MUSHROOMS.**

***OREGON STATE – MILAN HALL***

Drugs are fun; try 'em.

*– below –*

Brain Damage is for ever

*Washington State – Holland Library*

*U of Oregon – Lawrence Hall*

"Creative Devotion" might best describe the PAC Ten's pursuit of the spiritual.


THERE IS NO DEVIL; IT'S GOD WHEN HE'S DRUNK.

*UCLA – DODD HALL*


**Think God!**


*– below –*


**And in return, He might remember you too.**

*UCLA – Kinsey Hall*

98

*BELIEVE IN YOURSELF.*
*BELIEVE IN MANKIND.*
*BUT DON'T BE FOOLED; THERE IS NO GOD.*
                              *U OF WASHINGTON –*
                              *ODEGAARD LIBRARY*


**REALITY IS FOR THOSE WHO CAN'T HANDLE GOD.**
                              *U OF WASHINGTON – MUSIC*
                              *BUILDING*


If Man were meant to be, he would have been God.
                              *Arizona State – Art*


GOD IS DEAD, AND I WANT HIS JOB.
                              *U OF OREGON – PRINCE LUCIEN*
                              *CAMPBELL*


**Well, God's dead you know. But don't worry, Mary's
pregnant again.**

                              ***Washington State – Johnson
                              Tower***


*I AM A LONELY, DEPRESSED, ANXIOUS PERSON. WHAT
CAN I DO?*

                    *– BELOW –*

*LISTEN TO WHAT JESUS HAS TO SAY! YOU WON'T
REGRET IT.*

                    *– BELOW –*

*JUST AS SOON HAS HE TALKS TO ME, I'LL LISTEN.*
                    *U OF WASHINGTON –*
                    *ODEGAARD LIBRARY*


**JESUS LOVES YOU.**

### *– BELOW –*

**NO, HE LOVES *YOU*.**
                    ***U OF ARIZONA – ART***


Jesus loves you.

                *– below –*

And your wallet.
                    *LA International Airport*


JESUS LOVES YOU.

### *–BELOW –*

I'D RATHER HAVE MY WOMAN'S LOVE.
                    *WASHINGTON STATE – SCIENCE*
                    *AREA LIBRARY*


**No Jesus, no love.**
**Know Jesus, know love.**

                    ***U of Washington – Smith Hall***

*JESUS IS COMING!*

– BELOW –

*WON'T BE THE FIRST TIME.*

L.A. INTERNATIONAL AIRPORT

**JESUS DIED FOR YOUR SINS.**

*– BELOW –*

**I'M DYING FOR A LITTLE SIN OF MY OWN.**

***BERKELEY – EVANS HALL***

Long live Godlessness!

U of Washington – Eagleson Hall

DON'T BE NAIVE—GOD DOES PLAY FAVORITES.

U OF ARIZONA – SOCIAL SCIENCE

**"Who's God?" And if you can answer that one, "Whose God?"**

***U of Washington – Music Building***

*NATURE CREATED TIME SO THAT EVERYTHING WOULDN'T HAPPEN AT ONCE.*

– BELOW –

*DOES THAT MEAN THAT ONLY GOD CAN CALL 'TIME OUTS'?*

*STANFORD – MITCHELL HALL*


**IF GOD SAVES, CAN'T HE DO SOMETHING ABOUT THE WHALES?**

**USC – DOHENY LIBRARY**


God is one!

*Arizona State-Hayden Library*


THERE IS A GOD.

*– BELOW –*

MAN EVOLVED.

*– BELOW –*

THAT WAS HIS PLAN.

*U OF OREGON – SCIENCE MAIN BLOCK*


**God's master plan is to have mortals worry so much about the master plan that we neglect to make one of our own.**

***Berkeley – Doe Library***

102

*RIGHTEOUSNESS EXALTETH A NATION, BUT SIN IS A REPROACH TO ANY PEOPLE.*

*– BELOW –*

*THE MORAL MAJORITY SPEAKS!*

*– BELOW –*

*THIS ATTITUDE PROVES THAT A STANFORD EDUCATION CAN'T HELP EVERYONE.*

*STANFORD – MEYER LIBRARY*

**JOIN THE MORON MAJORITY.**

*U OF ARIZONA – PHYSICS*

God loves you anyway.

*Arizona State – Social Science*

LOVE YOUR ENEMIES. PRAY FOR THOSE WHO PERSECUTE YOU.

*WASHINGTON STATE – SCIENCE AREA LIBRARY*

**Make someone smile today.**

***Berkeley – Life Sciences***

*HAVE A NICE DAY!*

*– BELOW –*

*THIS IS THE ONLY NICE THING I'VE EVER SEEN ON THESE WALLS. WHAT ARE YOU, A FUCKIN' HOLY ROLLER?*
*U OF ARIZONA – MODERN LANGUAGES*

**HAVE A GOOD DAY. PLEASE, REALLY. I HOPE YOU DO. IT'S NOT HARD TO DO.**
***U OF ARIZONA – EDUCATION***

Reach out and touch a hand. Make a friend if you can.
*Stanford – Meyer Library*

WHAT HAVE YOU DONE TO MAKE SOMEONE HAPPY TODAY?
*BERKELEY – BOALDT LAW*

**Yes, God is alive and well.**

***– below –***

**I am alive and feeling so-so.**
***U of Arizona – Modern Languages***

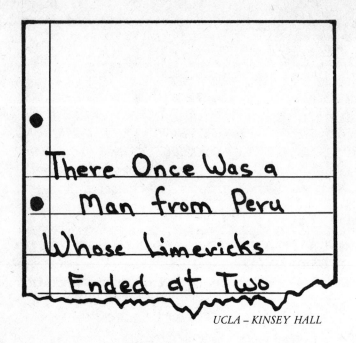

*There Once Was a Man from Peru Whose Limericks Ended at Two*

*UCLA – KINSEY HALL*

Most limericks in the PAC Ten come in a completed form. One sometimes feels that it would be better if a few of them did not.

**THERE ONCE WAS A MAN FROM ALGIERS**
**WHOSE DIET CONSISTED OF BEERS.**
**HE DRANK A SCHLUDWEILER**
**AND PROCLAIMED, "NOTHING'S VILER.**
**THIS STUFF'S EVEN TOO BAD FOR QUEERS."**

*OREGON STATE – WENIGER HALL*

There once was a young man from Leeds
who swallowed a packet of seeds.
Great tufts of grass
sprouted out of his ass
and his balls were all covered with weeds.

*UCLA – Kinsey Hall*

104

A MATHEMATICIAN NAMED HALL
HAD A HEXANGULAR BALL.
THE CUBE OF ITS WEIGHT,
TIMES HIS PRICK, PLUS EIGHT,
IS HIS PHONE NUMBER, GIVE HIM A CALL

*BERKELEY – BOALDT LAW*


There once was a man from Coblenz
the size of whose balls were immense.
One day playing soccer
he sprang his left knocker
and kicked it right over the fence.

*Stanford – Meyer Library*


A YOUNG VIOLINIST FROM RIO
SEDUCED A FINE CELLIST NAMED CLEO.
AS HE PULLED OFF HER PANTIES
SHE SAID, "NO ANDANTE'S.
I WANT THIS ALLEGRO CON BRIO!"

*UCLA – KINSEY HALL*


THERE ONCE WAS A MAN FROM HONG KONG
WHO HAD FINGERS THAT WERE SKINNY AND LONG.
HE ATE RICE WITH HIS FINGERS,
AND THE TASTE OF IT LINGERS.
BUT NOW ALL HIS FINGERS ARE GONE.

*U OF ARIZONA – MODERN*
*LANGUAGES*

There once was a man from Berlin
who didn't know his ass from his chin
When it came time to eat
beans were his treat
so his farts were the same as his grin.

*Oregon State – Weiniger Hall*


THERE ONCE WAS A MAN NAMED SWEENEY
WHO SPILLED SOME GIN ON HIS WEENIE.
JUST TO BE COUTH,
HE ADDED VERMOUTH,
AND SLIPPED HIS GIRLFRIEND A MARTINI.

*BERKELEY – BOALDT LAW*


**There once was a lady named Bright**
**who travelled much faster than light.**
**She took off one day.**
**in a relative way,**
**and returned the previous night.**

***Arizona State – Architecture***


*THERE WAS A YOUNG GIRL FROM ABERYSTWITH*
*WHO TOOK GRAIN TO THE MILL TO GET GRIST WITH.*
*THE MILLER'S SON, JACK.*
*LAID HER FLAT ON HER BACK,*
*AND UNITED THE ORGANS THEY PISSED WITH.*

*UCLA – KINSEY HALL*

THERE ONCE WERE THREE LADIES FROM BIRMINGHAM,
AND THIS IS THE STORY CONCERNING 'EM.
THEY LIFTED THE FROCK
AND TICKLED THE COCK
OF THE BISHOP WHO WAS CONFIRMING 'EM.

NOW THE BISHOP WAS NOBODY'S FOOL.
HE'D GONE TO A GREAT PUBLIC SCHOOL.
SO, HE LOWERED THEIR BRITCHES,
AND BUGGERED THOSE BITCHES
WITH HIS EIGHT INCH EPISCOPAL TOOL.

BUT THE LAST OF THE THREE (NAMED 'KEW')
REMARKED AS THE BISHOP WITHDREW,
"THE VICAR WAS QUICKER
AND SLICKER AND THICKER
AND THREE INCHES LONGER THAN YOU."

*STANFORD – LAW*


There once was a young man from Belaird
whose timing was seriously impaired.
His limericks would tend.
to come to an end
suddenly . . .


*– below –*


But they were often repaired.

*U of Washington – Padelford Hall*

# This is a one-liner.

*WASHINGTON STATE – JOHNSON TOWER*

PAC Ten humor comes in many forms at the hand of the graffitiist.

**Necrophilia is never having to say you're sorry.**
**Berkeley – Dwinelle Hall**

*YOU KNOW WHAT THE ARABS SAY, "OH, WELL . . ."*
*U OF OREGON – SCIENCE II*

**AS LONG AS I'M IN CHARGE HERE WE WILL HAVE NO LEADERS.**

*UCLA – DODD HALL*

Don't let baldness go to your head.

*Berkeley – Evans Hall*

HOW DID A FOOL AND HIS MONEY GET TOGETHER IN THE FIRST PLACE?

*U OF ARIZONA – EDUCATION*

**Lassie kills chickens!**

***U of Oregon – Deady Hall***

*BULLWINKLE IS A DOPE!*

*STANFORD – UNION*

**HUMPTY DUMPTY WAS PUSHED!**

***U OF OREGON – DEADY HALL***

Al Hirt blows!

*Stanford – Union*

BE ALERT, THE WORLD NEEDS MORE LERTS.

*WASHINGTON STATE – WILSON HALL*

**I'd rather have a bottle in front of me than a pre-frontal lobotomy.**

***Classic on all campuses***

*QUESTION: WHAT'S THE DIFFERENCE BETWEEN U OF W TOILET PAPER AND SAND PAPER?*
*ANSWER: SAND PAPER HAS ONE SMOOTH SIDE.*

> *U OF WASHINGTON – SMITH HALL*

**QUESTION: WHAT DO YOU GET WHEN YOU CROSS AN ELEPHANT AND A FLOOZY?**
**ANSWER: A TWO-TON PICKUP.**

> ***U OF WASHINGTON – PHYSICS***

Question: Why do Baptists forbid fucking standing up?
Answer: They are afraid it will lead to dancing.

> *Stanford – Union.*

PLEASE DO NOT ABBREV.

> *UCLA – MELNITZ HALL*

**Mommy! Mommy! Daddy's on fire!**
**Quick, get the marshmallows!**

> ***Stanford – Mitchell Hall***

*NAPOLEON SAT HERE AND BLEW HIS BONAPARTE.*

> *U OF ARIZONA – PSYCHOLOGY*

**QUESTION: WHAT DID THE CHINESE POLITICIAN SAY?**
**ANSWER: ERECT ME.**

> ***U OF WASHINGTON – SUZZALLO LIBRARY***

Do you know why blondes have more fun?
Because they are easier to see in the dark.

*U of Arizona – Business and Public*
*Administration*

TED KENNEDY FOR LIFEGUARD.

*BERKELEY – DWINELLE HALL*

**Question: What is the most evil potato in the Universe?**
**Answer: Darth Tater.**

***Berkeley – Life Sciences***

*I'VE TOLD YOU A MILLIONS TIMES NOT TO*
*EXAGGERATE!*

*UCLA – MELNITZ HALL*

**I SNATCH KISSES AND VICE VERSA.**

***WASHINGTON STATE – JOHNSON***
***HALL***

Question: What's the difference between a sorority and a
circus?
Answer: A circus has cunning stunts.

*U of Arizona – Architecture*

QUESTION: WHAT SHOULD YOU DO IN CASE OF
FALLOUT?
ANSWER: USE SHORTER STROKES.

*WASHINGTON STATE – SCIENCE*
*AREA LIBRARY*

112

**Question: What do you call da Vinci's lover?**
**Answer: Moaning Lisa.**

*BILLY CARTER SUFFERS FROM PEANUTS ENVY.*

**HEY, GARBONZA, HOW YOU BEAN?**

Farrah can play with my faucet any day.

QUESTION: WHAT DO YOU GET WHEN YOU NUKE ITALY?
ANSWERS: DAY-GLO DAGOS.

**Question: Why is toilet paper like the USS Enterprise?**
**Answer: They both circle Uranus and wipe out the Klingons.**

*QUESTIONS: WHY DO THEY CALL CAMELS THE SHIPS OF THE DESERT?*
*ANSWER: BECAUSE THEY ARE FULL OF ARAB SEMEN.*

Question: What do you call the nurse with the dirty knees?
Answer: The head nurse.

*U of Arizona – Home Ec &*
*Business*


QUESTION: WHAT DO YOU GET WHEN YOU CROSS AN
ELEPHANT WITH A RHINO?
ANSWER: 'ELL IF I KNOW.

*U OF WASHINGTON – PHYSICS*


**DID YOU HEAR ABOUT THE WHORE ON ELECTION DAY?
SHE DIDN'T CARE WHO GOT IN.**

***STANFORD – MITCHELL HALL***


The trouble with Freud is that he didn't have a good analyst.

*UCLA – Franz Hall*


QUESTION: HOW MANY GRAD STUDENTS DOES IT
TAKE TO SCREW IN A LIGHT BULB?
ANSWER: ONLY ONE, BUT IT TAKES HIM NINE
YEARS.

*STANFORD – ENGLISH*


**Well, I've taken enough shits in here that I think that it's
time for me to write something.**

**I walked into a Chinese whorehouse and was prompted to
ask the prostitute if her virginity ran sideways. Whereupon she
answered, "Why, are you a harmonica player?"**

**(I never was good at telling jokes.)**

*– below –*

114

**I coulda gone a long time without hearing this.**

*Arizona State – Life Sciences*

*QUESTION: WHY DON'T POLLACKS EAT M&MS?*
*ANSWER: THEY TAKE TOO LONG TO PEEL.*

*U OF WASHINGTON – PHYSICS*

**QUESTION: WHAT POTATO PLAYS IN THE MARCHING BAND?**
**ANSWER: THE TUBER.**

*BERKELEY – LIFE SCIENCES*

Question: How do you break an Iranian's finger?
Answer: Punch him in the nose.

*UCLA – Franz Hall*

CINDERELLA HAS BEEN KICKED OUT OF DISNEYLAND. SHE WAS CAUGHT SITTING ON PINNOCHIO'S FACE YELLING, "TELL A LIE, BABY! TELL A LIE!"

*ARIZONA STATE – LIFE SCIENCES*

**Women must have been designed by engineers. Who else would have run a sewage treatment plant through a recreation area.**

*Washington State – Dana Hall*

*QUESTION: WHAT DO CLONES DO ON MOTHER'S DAY?*
*ANSWER: WATCH THE TUBE.*

*STANFORD – UNION*

**DESCARTE: TO DO IS TO BE.**
**NIETZSCHE: TO BE IS TO DO.**
**SINATRA: DO BE DO BE DO.**

*CLASSIC ON ALL CAMPUSES*

Did you hear about the Polish lesbian? She likes men.

*UCLA – Franz Hall*

QUESTION: WHAT ARE CHEERLEADERS?
ANSWER: ATHLETIC SUPPORTERS.

*BERKELEY – LIFE SCIENCES*

**Question: When do you slap a midget?**
**Answer: When he says, "Your hair smells terrific!"**

*Arizona State – Language &*
*Literature*

*QUESTION: WHAT'S THE DIFFERENCE BETWEEN A*
*WHORE WITH DIARRHEA AND AN EPILEPTIC CORNHUSKER?*
*ANSWER: AN EPILEPTIC CORN HUSKER SHUCKS*
*BETWEEN FITS.*

*U OF WASHINGTON – BALMER*
*HALL*

**QUESTION: WHAT DO YOU CALL A GAY IRISHMAN?**
**ANSWER: A GAY LICK.**

*BERKELEY – WURSTER HALL*

Question: What do you call the place where a rubber lives?
Answer: A condominium.

*Oregon State – Social Science*


YOU CAN LEAD A HORTICULTURE, BUT YOU CAN'T MAKE HER THINK.

*U OF WASHINGTON – MUSIC*


**King Kong had a big banana.**

***UCLA – Franz Hall***


*QUESTION: WHY IS PUBIC HAIR CURLY?*
*ANSWER: IF IT WERE STRAIGHT IT WOULD POKE YOU IN THE EYES.*

*BERKELEY – KROEBER HALL*


**QUESTION: WHAT DO YOU CALL A CZECHOSLOVAKIAN ABORTION?**
**ANSWER: A CANCELLED CZECH.**

***U OF ARIZONA – PSYCHOLOGY***


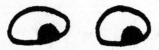


Just because you're paranoid doesn't mean they're not watching you.

*U of Washington – Architecture*

AYN RAND IS MILTON FRIEDMAN IN DRAG.

*STANFORD – UNION*


**If it weren't for Venetian blinds it would be curtains for everyone.**

***Berkeley – Evans Hall***


*DON'T WAIT, PROCRASTINATE NOW!*

*U OF ARIZONA – PSYCHOLOGY*


**GRAPE NUTS IS A SOCIAL DISEASE.**

***ARIZONA STATE – LIFE SCIENCES***

**(ferrous wheel)**

*U of Arizona – Psychology*

*(Mercedes Benzene)*

*U OF ARIZONA – PSYCHOLOGY*

**Two friends having dinner on Pluto:**
**1st: Well, what do you think of this place?**
**2nd: Oh, I don't know, it lacks atmosphere.**

*Berkeley – Wurster Hall*

Out of the abundance
of the heart (or lack
thereof) does the mouth
speak.

*STANFORD – LAW*

... and does the pen write. The hearts of the PAC Ten do indeed abound.

**TRUTH HITS EVERYBODY.**

*U OF WASHINGTON –*

*COMMUNICATIONS*

It takes a certain amount of wisdom to know you're a fool.

*– below –*

It takes a certain amount of fools to realize you're wise.

*U of Washington – Music*

119

120

FAILURE IS A MATTER OF OPINION.

*BERKELEY – DWINELLE HALL*

**Some people think they're being envied when they are really being pitied.**

*U of Oregon – Prince Lucien Campbell*

*OBJECTIVITY IS A DIRECTION, NOT A GOAL.*

*U OF WASHINGTON – ODEGAARD LIBRARY*

**NORMALITY IS DEPENDENT.**

*WASHINGTON STATE – HOLLAND LIBRARY*

Apathy is the opiate of the soul.

*U of Washington – Music*

REACH OUT AND GAIN, AS YOU WILL.

*ARIZONA STATE – ART*

**Dare to struggle! Dare to win!**

*U of Washington – Communications*

*WHY, EVERY TIME YOU'RE UP, DOES THE WORLD*
*TURN AROUND AND KICK YOU DOWN?*

> *U OF WASHINGTON – DENNY*
> *HALL*

**WILL BREAKS IRON—CREATE FREELY.**

> ***ARIZONA STATE – ART***

They say that money can't buy love in this world.

> *U of Washington – Smith Hall*

MONEY TALKS, BULLSHIT WALKS. AND SMALL
CHANGE RIDES THE BUS.

> *U OF WASHINGTON – SUZZALLO*
> *LIBRARY*

**I know that this is a hard habit to break, but you should
really try to communicate.**

> ***U of Arizona – Education***

*SOW A THOUGHT, REAP AN ACT.*
*SOW AN ACT, REAP A HABIT.*
*SOW A HABIT, REAP A LIFE STYLE*
*SOW A LIFE STYLE, REAP A DESTINY.*

> *U OF WASHINGTON – SAVERY*
> *HALL*

**ALL IS FOR THE BEST IN THIS THE BEST OF ALL POSSIBLE WORLDS.**

*ARIZONA STATE – ART*

We all must be given the liberty that we defend.

*Stanford – Meyer Library*

THE MEEK SHALL INHERIT THE EARTH. THE REST OF US SHALL ESCAPE TO THE STARS.

*U OF WASHINGTON – BALMER HALL*

**Love me while I am here, for I may never pass this way again.**

*U of Washington – Suzzallo Library*

*LIVE YOUR LIFE IN SUCH A WAY THAT EVEN THE UNDERTAKER REGRETS YOUR PASSING.*

*U OF ARIZONA – EDUCATION*

**LIVE EVERY MINUTE!**

*WASHINGTON STATE – FINE ARTS*

God gave us two ends—one to think with and one to sit on. Our success is determined by which end we use most. Which end are you using?

*U of Washington – Odegaard Library*

123

IF YOU CAN THINK OF IT, YOU HAVE DONE IT.

*BERKELEY – LIFE SCIENCES*

**Reason may dictate one thing, but you may dictate another.**

***U of Washington – Odegaard Library***

*WILDERNESS IS THE SALVATION OF THE WORLD.*

*WASHINGTON STATE – HOLLAND LIBRARY*

**JUDGE YOURSELF MORE AND OTHERS LESS.**

***U OF WASHINGTON – SUZZALLO LIBRARY***

Never attribute to malice that which is accurately explained by stupidity.

*U of Oregon – Allen Hall*

MOST PEOPLE ARE NEITHER AS GOOD NOR AS BAD AS YOUR FIRST IMPRESSION OF THEM.

*WASHINGTON STATE – VAN DOREN*

**Do unto others before they do unto you. Or, do unto others and then split.**

***U of Washington – Odegaard Library***

*Life is too short
to be serious,
and too long
to be funny.*

BERKELEY – EVANS HALL

Both the serious and the humorous in life are given full consideration.

**THE UNEXAMINED LIFE IS NOT WORTH LIVING.**

*U OF ARIZONA – EDUCATION*

Life is like a penis—when it's soft you can't beat it, but when it's hard you get fucked.

*Classic on all campuses*

LIFE IS LIKE A PINBALL—YOU EITHER RACK UP POINTS OR YOU LOSE YOUR BALLS.

*USC – DOHENY LIBRARY*

**Life is a cherrabowlies!**

*Washington State – Fine Arts*

*LIFE IS LIKE A SORORITY—ONE BITCH AFTER ANOTHER.*

*U OF ARIZONA – BIOLOGICAL
SCIENCES EAST*

**LIFE IS LIKE A SHIT SANDWICH—THE MORE BREAD YOU
HAVE, THE LESS SHIT YOU HAVE TO EAT.**

*CLASSIC ON ALL CAMPUSES*

Life is like a peanut butter and jelly sandwich—it is always
stuck to the roof of your mouth.

*Arizona State – Art*

LIFE IS LIKE WANDERING THROUGH A COW
PASTURE AT NIGHT—IT'S HARD TO GET ALL THE WAY
THROUGH WITHOUT STEPPING IN SOME SHIT.

*U OR OREGON – SCIENCE II*

**Life is like a dick—if you're in the hole, you're getting
fucked.**

*U of Washington – Suzzallo
Library*

*LIFE IS WHAT HAPPENS WHILE YOU'RE BUSY MAKING
OTHER PLANS.*

*U OF WASHINGTON – PHYSICS*

**LIFE IS LIKE A JOKE ... A BAD ONE AT THAT.**

*BERKELEY – UNION*

Life is like a toiletpaper roll—it keeps running out on you.

*U of Washington – Odegaard Library*

LIFE IS A DREAM. CHANGE YOUR MIND TO CHANGE YOUR LIFE.

*BERKELEY – UNION*

**Dreams are the essence of the mind ... escape.**

**Washington State – Holland**
**Library**

*DREAMS ARE WET.*

*WASHINGTON STATE –*
*HOLLAND LIBRARY*

**WELL, EXCUSE ME!**

**STANFORD – MITCHELL HALL**

Death is alive and well. It's our only hope.

*Berkeley – Dwinelle Hall*

EVERYBODY GONNA DIE. DON'T MATTER WHEN. DON'T MATTER WHY.

*BERKELEY – DWINELLE HALL*

127

There's nothing wrong with dying; people do it all the time.

*– below –*

But it's so tacky.

*Berkeley – Dwinelle Hall*


*IT'S A GAME.*
*THE END'S THE SAME.*

*U OF WASHINGTON – BALMER*
*HALL*


**SEASONS DON'T FEAR THE REAPER.**
**NOR DO THE WIND, THE SUN OR THE RAIN.**

*WASHINGTON STATE – JOHNSON*
*HALL*


Ain't no life nowhere.

*– below –*

Then kiss the sky!

*Arizona State – Art*


THE WEEDS WILL WIN IN THE END, OF COURSE.

*BERKELEY – EVANS HALL*

So...
we meet
again.

U OF OREGON – PRINCE LUCIEN
CAMPBELL

After all, what can one say?

**DON'T CRUSH THE DWARF; HAND ME THE PLIERS.**
*STANFORD – UNION*

No matter which way he goes, his shadow always knows.
*Stanford – Meyer Library*

NOT BIRD,
NOR TURD,
NOR EVEN FROG;
JUST A LITTLE OLD UNDERDOG.

*U OF WASHINGTON – SMITH
HALL*

**The world is one big baby farm.**

*U of Washington – Odegaard*
*Library*


*IF YOU SEE CHRIS W., LAUGH AT HIM FOR ME.*
*STANFORD – MEYER LIBRARY*


**NELSON EDDIE FOR US CONGRESS!**
**BERKELEY – DWINELLE HALL**


Where is Zarathustra when we need him?
*U of Washington – Denny Hall*

NO FOOL, TANYA TUCKER.
*U OF ARIZONA – ARCHITECTURE*


**For a good time, call Princess Margaret.**
*U of Arizona – Modern Languages*


*LOUISE IS NOT HALF BAD.*
*UCLA – GRADUATE SCHOOL OF*
*MANAGEMENT*


**JOIN THE CALIFORNIA BODIES FOR SCIENCE PROGRAM COURSE! CREDIT FOR EVERY BODY YOU RECRUIT! JOB PLACEMENT WITH TOP HOSPITAL GUARANTEED UPON GRADUATION!**
**BERKELEY – UNION**

Neanderthalism works!

*Berkeley – Dwinelle Hall*


THE ARTIST WHO CAN PAINT THE SUN MAKING
LOVE TO A HUMAN FORM HAS GRASPED THE
ONAGRAMMATIZED MARROW.

*UCLA – MACGOWAN HALL*


**Eschew terminological obfuscation!**

***Stanford – Meyer Library***


*A STROLLING CLONE LATHERS NO CROSS.*

*STANFORD – PHYSICS LECTURE*


**IF A LITTLE PLANT IS GENEROUS WITH YOU, YOU MUST
THANK HER, OR SHE WILL NOT LET YOU GO.**

***U OF WASHINGTON – MUSIC***


Lick the boots of fear, you runney nose twit!

*U of Washington – Balmer Hall*


YOU'RE A MEAN ONE, MR. GRINCH!

*BERKELEY – LIFE SCIENCES*


**Let's do the time warp again.**


*– below –*

I donwanna.

*U of Washington – Balmer Hall*


*I DON'T THINK WE'RE IN KANSAS ANYMORE, TOTO . . .*
*U OF OREGON – PRINCE LUCIEN CAMPBELL*


**FRIDAY WAS HERE!**

*U OF WASHINGTON – DENNY HALL*


Kilroy was here!

*Rainbow Room – Garden Grove, Ca.*


UNCLE WIGGLEY SLEPT HERE!

*BERKELEY – LECONTE HALL*


**Horrible Orville was here!**

*U of Washington – Savery Hall*


*GODOT WAS HERE, BUT YOU WILL PROBABLY NEVER BE ABLE TO PROVE IT.*

*STANFORD – UNION*


**FOR THOSE OF YOU WHO THOUGHT THAT I WAS GONE— WELL, I'M BACK.**

*– BELOW –*

132

**IS THAT YOU, MOM?**

*USC – WATT HALL*

Trotsky lives!

*Berkeley – Dwinelle Hall*

WILLY NELSON LIVES!

*OREGON STATE – KERR LIBRARY*

**Amin is alive and living in Newark!**

**U of Oregon – Lawrence Hall**

*FRODO LIVES!*

*ARIZONA STATE – ART*

**NEIL YOUNG LIVES FOREVER!**

**BERKELEY – MOFFIT LIBRARY**

Jefferson Airplaine lives!

*U of Washington – Suzzallo Library*

BUDDHA IS ALIVE AND MOWING LAWNS IN
PASADENA.

*U OF WASHINGTON – GOULD
HALL*

I'm telling you now, I'm gonna write a best-seller within the next five years.

*USC – Watt Hall*

*FLATTERIZE AND SATIRIZE!*

*BERKELEY – UNION*

**WHY WARTS???**

***BERKELEY – LIFE SCIENCES***

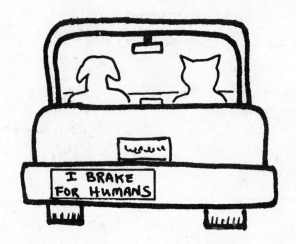

*U of Oregon – Science II*

I ONCE WAS AN ITALIAN CAR.

*OREGON STATE – WENIGER HALL*

**Salvage pelicans!**

***Berkeley – Union***

134

*ONE GOOD TERN DESERVES ANOTHER.*
*BERKELEY – WHEELER HALL*

**SHEEP ARE ANIMAL SEX OBJECTS.**
***ARIZONA STATE – EDUCATION***

Support vegetarians! Lettuce be friends!
*UCLA – Melnitz Hall*

CARNIVORES EAT MEAT!
*UCLA – KINSEY HALL*

**In the world of mules
there are no rules.**

***U of Oregon – Science II***

*FREE PUPPIES!*

*U OF WASHINGTON – SMITH
HALL*

**FREE THE SAN FRANCISCO 49ERS!**
***U OF WASHINGTON –
COMMUNICATIONS***

Free the Boaldt 900!

*Berkeley – Boaldt Law*

FREE THE TOPS 200
  IBM 370
  HP 3000
  MOS 6502
  MOTOROLA 68000

*STANFORD – CENTER OF
EDUCATION RESEARCH*

**Live it, or live without it.**

*Oregon State – Agriculture Hall*

*WE'RE ALL BOZOS IN THIS STALL.*

*STANFORD – UNION*

**THE RAIN IN SPAIN FALLS MAINLY ON THE PLAIN.
SPAIN'S RAIN IS MAINLY PLAIN.**

*STANFORD – UNION*

Make the leap to nothingness!

*Stanford – Union*


THERE WILL BE AN ORGANIZATIONAL MEETING OF
ANARCHISTS TUESDAY EVENING.

*U OF ARIZONA – MODERN*
*LANGUAGES*


**Anarchists unite! You have nothing to lose but your
ideology.**

**Washington State – Johnson
Tower**


*NIHILISTS ARE WORTHLESS!*

*UCLA – SCHOENBERG HALL*


**CRIME DOES NOT PAY, EXCEPT WITH COMPUTERS.**

**WASHINGTON STATE – JOHNSON
TOWER**


60's nostalgia!

*Oregon State – Agriculture Hall*


LET'S GO BACK TO 1967 IN SAN FRANCISCO.

*– BELOW –*

FLOWER POWER!

> *U OF OREGON – PRINCE LUCIEN CAMPBELL*

**Left nostril quiet time.**

> ***Stanford – Mitchell Hall***

*TODAY I RAN THE INCH!*

> *STANFORD – UNION*

**THE CIGARETTE IS SCRATCHED! I WILL NOT BUY IT!**

> ***UCLA – KINSEY HALL***

Get lurdified!

> *UCLA – Kinsey Hall*

TRIANGLES ARE SIMPLICITY OF PERFECTION.

> *OREGON STATE – MILAN HALL*

**I was sitting here in May 1980 when the mountain blew its top.**

> ***Washington State – Fine Arts***

*NUKE ST. HELENS!*

– BELOW –

138

*ST. HELENS NUKED US.*

> *U OF OREGON – GILBERT HALL*

**HELEN IS AN ASH-HOLE.**

> ***OREGON STATE – MILAN HALL***

Helen forgot to take her Earth-control pills.

> *Washington State – Science Area Library*

WHEN E. F. HUTTON TALKS, PEOPLE ARE PARALIZED.

> *BERKELEY – DWINELLE HALL*

**In case of a Big Mac attack . . .**

> ***U of Washington – Electrical Engineering***

*COPENHAGEN SATISFIES.*

> *WASHINGTON STATE – JOHNSON HALL*

**WE CAN'T ESCAPE FROM ADVERTISING.**

> ***BERKELEY – DWINELLE HALL***

TODAY IS LIKE A LONG SIGH ...

**Pernickety nigpusses must be killed in their shoes where they live.**

*IT'S THE MUD*
*IT'S THE MUD—*
*THAT MAKES IT A MUD SHARK.*

**GOD-DAMNED GAWKIN' GARGOYLES!**

Those pajama people are driving me crazy.

PLEASE DON'T SQUEEZE THE FLEXOPUMPS.

*BERKELEY – ARCHITECTURE*

**Why are loxodantas always so cute?**

***Berkeley – Evans Hall***

*ARMADILLO AWARENESS!*

*WASHINGTON STATE – SLOAN
HALL*

**I WANNA GO HOME TO THE ARMADILLOS.**

***– BELOW –***

**UP AGAINST THE WALL, REDNECK MOTHERS!**

***U OF OREGON – SCIENCE MAIN
BLOCK***

And slime had they for mortar!

*Stanford – Meyer Library*

I THINK WE ARE IN RAT'S ALLEY WHERE THE DEAD MEN LOST THEIR BONES.

*U OF OREGON – SCIENCE II*


**Shoot pictures!**

*U of Washington – Savery Hall*


*DO RANDOM ACTS!*

*UCLA – MELNITZ HALL*


**THERE'S A CRACK IN THE COSMIC EGG.**

***UCLA – GEOLOGY***


Have you seen the little piggies?

*Washington State – Fullmer*


HI, KIDS!

*U OF ARIZONA – MODERN LANGUAGES*


**Can you say 'Wimpy'?**

***Arizona State – Art***

*ONLY FLAWED HUMAN SPECIMENS REQUIRE
CHEMICAL ALTERATION*

*—MEAN JOE GREENE*
*ARIZONA STATE – PHYSICAL
SCIENCE*

**A LITTLE TOO MUCH OF EVERYTHING IS JUST ABOUT
RIGHT.**

**USC – VON KLEINSMID CENTER**

Pervert your sense of decorum.

*Berkeley – Wurster Hall*

GOODBYE, BLUE MONDAY.

*U OF WASHINGTON –
ODEGAARD LIBRARY*

**Sometimes the wolves are silent and the moon howls.**

*– below –*

**. . . and sometimes not.**

*– below –*

**You didn't understand.**

*– below –*

And sometimes when moons and wolves are silent, I'm left to howl alone. (Did I understand, Master?)

*USC – Mudd Hall of Philosphy*

*BOOM . . . BOOM . . . OUT GO THE LIGHTS!*

*WASHINGTON STATE – SCIENCE HALL*

We ain't done yet !!!

Well, there you have it. We have preserved the culture of the PAC Ten. It will live beyond that time when Nature decides to take back that which she has given. We think that those who scoffed were wrong. We think that it was worth it.

In fact, we were quite impressed with the universities of the PAC Ten, so much so that we noted numerous characteristics for which individual schools could be proud.

These honors might normally be reserved for the future, to be bestowed eulogistically at the demise of the receiver. We felt that inappropriate.

Although their end may be imminent, we nevertheless felt that the PAC Ten schools should not be asked to wait for their reward. They have earned the right to be honored now. Therefore, we have recognized the following distinctions and honors.

To Berkeley: Our thanks for preserving the entire counter-culture of the '60s virtually intact.

To UCLA: Recognition for the most distinguished parking facilities and for the most original use of uniformed parking attendants.

To Stanford: An award for being the only school where the morning after finds the student terrace littered with half-empty Perrier bottles.

To Arizona State: An award for the fashionability of the squint.

There were not nearly the number of sunglasses worn as called for by the sun's intensity in Phoenix.

To U of Washington: An award for massiveness of structure. (The winner of this award was closely followed by runner-up, Berkeley.)

To USC: We honor USC with this question: "Is possession of a tennis racket a prerequisite for admission to USC?"

To Oregon State: An award for the best student-union reading room, combined with an award for the best impersonation of a hunting lodge by a student-union reading room.

To U of Washington: An award for the most ducks in their fountain.

To U of Arizona and Arizona State: A combined award for the best facilities for the handicapped.

To Stanford: An award for the most effective and nastiest traffic barriers.

To Stanford: An award for the largest collection of used automobile oil pans. (We did not actually see this collection, but given the effectiveness of the previously honored barriers, we assume that there is a significant collection.)

To U of Oregon: An award for the most fog. We understand that this award would often be more appropriately bestowed upon U of Washington. However, such was not the case during our research.

This series of awards completes our research in the PAC Ten. We will now sit back with our daily newspaper and await the headlines about the eruption, the earthquake, or the drought. Until then, enjoy!

# KNOCK YOUR SOCKS OFF!!!

# See what other campuses are up to from the *inside*!!

### GRAFFITI IN THE IVY LEAGUE
(and thereabouts)

Looking for the Northeast universities' secrets of success, our researchers probed past the ivy-covered halls to the scrawl-covered walls. They selected from the genius graffiti the significant, the symbolic, the succinct and the smutty. Now, it's up to you to crack the codes or crack up reading GRAFFITI IN THE IVY LEAGUE (and thereabouts).

available in quality paperback

V37602-7

### GRAFFITI IN THE SOUTHWEST CONFERENCE

Is it true folks are friendlier in the Southwest? Our researchers set out to tour the Southwest conference universities to find out. Their report: there's a lot of smiling going on, but it just might be graffiti-itis, an irresistible upturning of the mouth that is an allergic response to some of the funniest toilet wall wit we've ever collected.

A Warner quality paperback

V37604-3

### GRAFFITI IN THE BIG TEN

To gather these immortal scrawlings our researchers penetrated to the ultimate inner sancta—the toilet stalls—plumbing the very depths of the thinking of students at the universities of the Upper Midwest. Here is the collection—profane, profound and profuse. And FUNNY!!

A Warner quality paperback

V37504-7

Each book priced at $4.95.

## SHARE YOUR FAVORITE GRAFFITI WITH US.

No purchase is necessary to qualify. Simply send in your favorite pieces of graffiti on a 3 x 5 index card along with the source of your pieces (for example, campus building and name of school). If they are used in forthcoming sequels of our graffiti books, you will be notified and sent a free copy of our next great book.

Send to: **Reader's Favorite Graffiti**
**Brown House Galleries**
**P. O. Box 4243**
**Madison, WI    53711**

Submission of favorite graffiti by readers constitutes your permission for accepted graffiti to be published in any sequels.

—Marina N. Haan
—Richard B. Hammerstrom